The
YOUNGER
IRISH
POETS

The
YOUNGER
IRISH
POETS

edited by
Gerald Dawe

The
Blackstaff
Press

British Library Cataloguing in Publication Data

The Younger Irish poets.
  1. English poetry – 20th century
  I. Dawe, Gerald
  821'.914'08   PR1225

  ISBN 0–85640–261–3

First published by The Blackstaff Press Limited in 1982
with the assistance of The Arts Council of Northern Ireland
Reprinted in 1983 by The Blackstaff Press Limited
3 Galway Park, Dundonald, Belfast BT16 0AN

Printed in Northern Ireland
by Belfast Litho Printers Limited

CONTENTS

EDITOR'S NOTE

In 1962 John Montague and Thomas Kinsella edited *The Dolmen Miscellany of Irish Writing*. Their brief preface referred to a 'new generation of writers' who reflected, in the editors' estimation, 'a general change of sensibility' which the *Miscellany* sought to represent. My aim in this anthology is similar to theirs.

I see this anthology as a record of the work of a number of Irish poets born within just over a decade of one another (1944–56), whose writing came to prominence in the latter half of the 1970s. The poets are presented in terms of this common denominator – chronologically in regard to each other, and generally in regard to their own published work.

The anthology lays no claim to being comprehensive. It is, I trust, representative of the various strands that go to make up contemporary Irish poetry written in the English language. The poets themselves come from north, south, east and west of the country; their backgrounds are equally diverse: Protestant, Catholic, urban, and rural. Some of them no longer live in Ireland – Paulin, Peskett, Ryan, Maxton, and Sweeney – while others live in various parts of the country – Belfast, Dublin, Cork, and Galway.

Some of the poets, at quite an early stage in their writing careers, have established a reputation outside Ireland. This is particularly true of poets from the North. The reasons, notwithstanding individual merit, of course, are inevitably historical and bound up with the social and political bonds which tie Northern Ireland to Britain.

Of the poets born in the South of Ireland included in this anthology, few have sought, to my knowledge, recognition outside their country. Yet their work has not received, inside Ireland, the attention I believe it deserves. This anthology is an attempt to right that imbalance and in so doing bring to a wider audience both the achievement to date and the promise of the younger contemporary Irish poets.

In many ways, the focus of critics and readers of Irish poetry has been directed at the North, with evaluations being made of the effects 'The Troubles' have had upon creative writing there. This kind of attention has created its own problems. Coming to creative self-awareness during a period of intense sectarian strife may compel the younger Northern writer to forge a protective rhetoric of equivocation. This may in turn distort the inherent growth of his or her vision by confining it to the immediate, domesticated present. Perhaps, though, it is unfair to expect anything more in the circumstances and garrulous to force the point.

Alternatively, the 1970s may have led some poets, as Samuel Beckett once remarked in a review of Irish poetry in 1934, to 'a flight from self-awareness' and to accept what he called 'an accredited theme . . . where the self is either most happily obliterated or else so improved and enlarged that it can be mistaken for part of the décor . . .' Time will tell.

It is my opinion that all the poets included in this anthology demonstrate, in their search for what makes sense over and against the inherited, given meanings of Irish history, north and south, an independence from any 'accredited theme'. The flight is not from self-awareness but rather a tentative returning to it, discovering *en route* what matters in this day and age, and what freedoms are actually available to us.

In other words, the poets presented here are finding ways to liberate themselves, their art, and, by implication alone, their readers, from the literary conventions and literal expectations that have been handed down from the past. Present, I feel, in their best work is a need to unburden themselves of the past through whatever means, traditional or experimental, that sustains their own imaginative responsibilities.

I have selected what I think is a diverse and contrasting range of expression. I would have liked to include in this anthology a poet working in the Irish language. My own limitations, however, and restrictions on size prohibited me from doing so, while publications such as *Innti* and *The Writers* (O'Brien Press) suggest that Irish language poets are now being catered for with professional care.

Gerald Dawe
Galway 1982

PAUL DURCAN

Paul Durcan was born in Dublin in 1944, of
Mayo parents. He studied Archaeology and
Medieval History at University College,
Cork. In 1974 he won the Patrick Kavanagh
Award and received Arts Council Bursaries in
1976 and 1980.

Publications:
Endsville, with Brian Lynch, New Writers
Press, 1967
O Westport in the Light of Asia Minor,
Dublin Magazine Press, 1975
Teresa's Bar, Gallery Press, 1976
Sam's Cross, Profile Press, 1978
Jesus, Break His Fall, Raven Arts Press, 1980

November 1967

to Katherine

I awoke with a pain in my head
And my mother standing at the end of the bed;
'There's bad news in the paper,' she said,
'Patrick Kavanagh is dead.'

After a week which was not real
At last I settled down to a natural meal;
I was sitting over a pint and a beef sandwich
In Mooney's across the street from the Rotunda.

By chance I happened to tune in
To the conversation at the table from me;
I heard an old Northsider tell to his missus,
'He was pure straight; God rest him; not like us.'

The weeping headstones of the Isaac Becketts

The Protestant graveyard was a forbidden place
So naturally as children we explored its precincts;
Clambered over drystone walls under elms and chestnuts,
Parted long grasses and weeds, poked about under yews,
Reconnoitred the chapel whose oak doors were always closed,
Stared at the schist headstones of the Isaac Becketts.
And then we would depart with mortal sins in our bones
As ineradicable as an arthritis
But we had seen enough to know what the old folks meant
When we would overhear them whisperingly at night refer to

'The headstones of the Becketts – they would make you weep'.
These arthritises of sin –
But although we had only six years each on our backs
We could decipher
Brand-new roads open up through heaven's fields
And upon them – like thousands upon thousands
Of people kneeling in the desert –
The weeping headstones of the Isaac Becketts.

The girl with the keys to Pearse's Cottage

to John and Judith Meagher

When I was sixteen I met a dark girl;
Her dark hair was darker because her smile was so bright;
She was the girl with the keys to Pearse's Cottage;
And her name was Cait Killann.

The cottage was built into the side of a hill;
I recall two windows and cosmic peace
Of bare brown rooms and on whitewashed walls
Photographs of the passionate and pale Pearse.

I recall wet thatch and peeling jambs
And how all was best seen from below in the field;
I used sit in the rushes with ledger-book and pencil
Compiling poems of passion for Cait Killann.

Often she used linger on the sill of a window;
Hands by her side and brown legs akimbo;
In sun-red skirt and moon-black blazer;
Looking toward our strange world wide-eyed.

3

Our world was strange because it had no future;
She was America-bound at summer's end.
She had no choice but to leave her home –
The girl with the keys to Pearse's Cottage.

O Cait Killann, O Cait Killann,
You have gone with your keys from your own native place.
Yet here in this dark – El Greco eyes blaze back
From your Connemara postman's daughter's proudly mortal face.

What is a Protestant, Daddy?

Gaiters were sinister
And you dared not
Glance up at the visage;
It was a long lean visage
With a crooked nose
And beaked dry lips
And streaky gray hair
And they used scurry about
In small black cars
(Unlike Catholic bishops
Stately in big cars
Or Pope Pius XII
In his gold-plated Cadillac)
And they'd make dashes for it
Across deserted streets
And disappear quickly
Into vast cathedrals
All silent and aloof,
Forlorn and leafless,
Their belfry louvres
Like dead men's lips,
And whose congregations, if any,

Were all octogenarian
With names like Iris;
More likely
There were no congregations
And these rodent-like clergymen
Were conspirators;
You could see it in their faces;
But as to what the conspiracies
Were about, as children
We were at a loss to know;
Our parents called them 'parsons'
Which turned them from being rodents
Into black hooded crows
Evilly flapping their wings
About our virginal souls;
And these 'parsons' had wives –
As unimaginable a state of affairs
As it would have been to imagine
A pope in a urinal;
Protestants were Martians
Light-years more weird
Than zoological creatures;
But soon they would all go away
For as a species they were dying out.
Soon there would be no more Protestants. . .
O Yea, O Lord,
I was a proper little Irish Catholic boy
Way back in the 1950s.

Going home to Mayo, Winter, 1949

Leaving behind us the alien, foreign city of Dublin
My father drove through the night in an old Ford Anglia,
His five-year-old son in the seat beside him,
The rexine seat of red leatherette,
And a yellow moon peered in through the windscreen.
'Daddy, Daddy,' I cried, 'Pass out the moon,'
But no matter how hard he drove he could not pass out the moon.
Each town we passed through was another milestone
And their names were magic passwords into eternity:
Kilcock, Kinnegad, Strokestown, Elphin,
Tarmonbarry, Tulsk, Ballaghaderreen, Ballavarry;
Now we were in Mayo and the next stop was Turlough,
The village of Turlough in the heartland of Mayo,
And my father's mother's house, all oil-lamps and women,
And my bedroom over the public bar below,
And in the morning cattle-cries and cock-crows:
Life's seemingly seamless garment gorgeously rent
By their screeches and bellowings. And in the evenings
I walked with my father in the high grass down by the river
Talking with him – an unheard-of thing in the city.

But home was not home and the moon could be no more outflanked
Than the daylight nightmare of Dublin city:
Back down along the canal we chugged into the city
And each lock-gate tolled our mutual doom;
And railings and palings and asphalt and traffic-lights,
And blocks after blocks of so-called 'new' tenements –
Thousands of crosses of loneliness planted
In the narrowing grave of the life of the father;
In the wide, wide cemetery of the boy's childhood.

Poetry, a natural thing

Basking salmon under the salmon bridge at Galway
or, a deer at a window-sill of Magdalen College
being fed bread-crumbs by my friend Michael Lurgan –
It was October and he was reading Proust
and I was an inmate of a London hostel for homeless boys

Where I shared a room with a boy from Blackpool
whose silence was the silence of a bear in a cave
and who had a passion for looking at himself in the looking-glass:
I had the feeling that he had the makings of a policeman
and that one day he would truncheon somebody to death.

But basking salmon of self-sufficiency or, supplicant deer,
or, answers to questions, always remain:
It is not I who am hiding in the trees from my father:
it is he who is hiding in the trees, and he is waiting to ambush me
as I step out the bright forest path to the spring.

That's poetry, a natural thing.

Backside to the wind

A fourteen-year-old boy is out rambling alone
By the scimitar shores of Killala Bay
And he is dreaming of a French Ireland
Backside to the wind.

What kind of village would I now be living in?
French vocabularies intertwined with Gaelic
And Irish women with French fathers
Backside to the wind.

The Ballina Road would become the Rue de Humbert
And wine would be the staple drink of the people;
A staple diet of potatoes and wine
Backsides to the wind.

Monsieur O'Duffy might be the harbour-master
And Madame Duffy the mother of thirteen
Tiny philosophers to overthrow Maynooth
Backsides to the wind.

And Father Molloy might be a worker-priest
Up to his knees in manure at the cattle-mart;
And dancing and loving on the streets at evening
Backsides to the wind.

Jean Arthur Rimbaud might have grown up here
In a hillside terrace under the round tower;
Would he, like me, have dreamed of an Arabian Dublin
Backside to the wind?

And Garda Ned MacHale might now be a gendarme
Having hysterics at the crossroads;
Excommunicating male motorists, ogling females
Backsides to the wind.

I walk on, facing the village ahead of me,
A small concrete oasis in the wild countryside;
Not the embodiment of the dream of a boy
Backside to the wind.

Seagulls and crows, priests and nuns,
Perch on the rooftops and steeples,
And their Anglo-American mores are killing me
Backside to the wind.

Not to mention the Japanese invasion:
Blunt people as serious as ourselves
And as humourless; money is our God
Backsides to the wind.

The ancient Franciscan Friary of Moyne
Stands nobly, roofless, by;
Past it rolls a vast concrete pipe
Backside to the wind

Carrying out chemical waste to sea
From the Asahi synthetic-fibre plant;
Where once monks sang, wage-earners slave
Backsides to the wind.

Yet somehow, sweet River Moy,
Run on though I end my song;
You are the vestments of the salmon of learning
Backside to the wind.

But I have no choice but to leave, to leave,
And yet there is nowhere I more yearn to live
Than in my own wild countryside
Backside to the wind.

Making love outside Áras An Uachtaráin*

When I was a boy, myself and my girl
Used bicycle up to the Phoenix Park;
Outside the gates we used lie in the grass
Making love outside Áras An Uachtaráin.

Often I wondered what De Valera would have thought
Inside in his ivory tower
If he knew that we were in his green, green grass
Making love outside Áras An Uachtaráin.

Because the odd thing was – oh how odd it was –
We both revered Irish patriots
And we dreamed our dreams of a green, green flag
Making love outside Áras An Uachtaráin.

But even had our names been Diarmaid and Gráinne
We doubted De Valera's approval
For a poet's son and a judge's daughter
Making love outside Áras An Uachtaráin.

I see him now in the heat-haze of the day
Blindly stalking us down;
And, levelling an ancient rifle, he says 'Stop
Making love outside Áras An Uachtaráin.'

* President's Mansion

In memory: The Miami Showband: massacred 31 July 1975

Beautiful are the feet of them that preach the gospel of peace,
Of them that bring glad tidings of good things

In a public house, darkly-lit, a patriotic (sic)
Versifier whines into my face: 'You must take one side
Or the other, or you're but a fucking romantic'.
His eyes glitter hate and ambition, porter and whiskey,
And I realize that he is blind to the braille connection
Between a music and a music-maker.
'You must take one side or the other
Or you're but a fucking romantic':
The whine is icy
And his eyes hang loose like sheets from poles
On a bare wet hillside in winter
And his mouth gapes like a cave in ice;

10

It is a whine in the crotch of whose fear
Is fondled a dream-gun blood-smeared;
It is in war – not poetry or music –
That men find their niche, their glory hole;
Like most of his fellows
He will abide no contradiction in the mind:
He whines: 'If there is birth, there cannot be death'
And – jabbing a hysterical forefinger into my nose and eyes –
'If there is death, there cannot be birth'.
Peace to the souls of those who unlike my confrère
Were true to their trade
Despite death-dealing blackmail by fanatics and racists:
You made music, and that was all: You were realists
And beautiful were your feet.

Death in the quadrangle

I stand here in a quadrangle – which is worse than
        in a quandary:
At least in a quandary you don't know where you are:
But here in a quadrangle I know the angle
And that is my pain, that is why I linger alone
Knowing only loneliness to the bone
Up the shaking stairs of the falling years:
If only I did not know the angle,
If only I was that boy there from behind the Mountain,
Or that girl there from Another Country –
But I am me – like most of us I am me –
And like most of us I stand here in a quadrangle
        not knowing
Where to go or in whom to confide my experience
        of the tyranny

11

Of these privileged pedagogues who pedal perjury
Term after term after term in the courts of truth:
O Erasmus, Jesus: down dying, we dreamed of Ruth
    amidst the alien corn.

Pwofessor O'Bwien, dthon'th you think these
    swudents are exweemly uncouth?
This mworning I hadth to shooth one dwead in the
    quadwangle – in my sweminar
He hadth the nwerve to mention the word 'Twuth':
    Fancy that! Twuth!

For My Lord Tennyson I Shall Lay Down My Life

for Anthony Cronin

Here at the Mont St Michel of my master,
At the horn of beaches outside Locksley Hall,
On the farthest and coldest shore,
In the June day under pain of night,
I keep at my mind to make it say,
Make it say, make it say,
As his assassins make for me,
The pair of them revolving nearer and nearer
(And yet, between breaths, farther and farther),
Make it say:
'For My Lord Tennyson I Shall Lay Down My Life.'

I say that – as nearer and nearer they goosestep:
Vanity: and *Gloom* not far behind.
'For My Lord Tennyson I Shall Lay Down My Life.'

The death by heroin of Sid Vicious

There – but for the clutch of luck – go I.

At daybreak – in the arctic fog of a February
    daybreak –
Shoulderlength helmets in the watchtowers of the
    concentration camp
Caught me out in the intersecting arcs of the
    swirling searchlights:

There were at least a zillion of us caught out there
– Like   ladybirds   under   a   boulder   –
But under the microscope each of us was unique,

Unique and we broke for cover, crazily breasting
The barbed wire and some of us made it
To the forest edge, but many of us did not

Make it, although their unborn children did –
Such as you whom the camp commandant branded
Sid Vicious of the Sex Pistols. Jesus, break his fall:

There – but for the clutch of luck – go we all.

February 1979

EAVAN BOLAND

Eavan Boland was born in Dublin in 1944
and was educated in London, New York, and
Trinity College, Dublin, where she taught for
a time. In 1968 she received the Macaulay
Fellowship for poetry.

Publications:
New Territory, Allen Figgis, 1967
The War Horse, Victor Gollancz, 1975
In Her Own Image, Arlen House, 1980
Night Feed, Arlen House, 1982

Critical works:
W. B. Yeats and His World
(with Micheál Mac Liammóir),
Thames and Hudson, 1971

Belfast Vs. Dublin

for Derek Mahon

Into this city of largesse
You carried clever discontent,
And now, the budget of your time here spent,
Let us not mince the word: this is no less
Than halfway towards the end. Gathering
In a rag tied to a stick, all in confusion,
Dublin reverence and Belfast irony—
Now hoist with your conclusion.

Cut by the throats before we spoke
One to another, yet we breast
The dour line of North and South, pressed
Into action by the clock. Here we renounce
All dividend except the brilliant quarrel
Of our towns: mine sports immoral
Courtiers in unholy waste, but your unwitty
Secret love for it is Belfast city.

We have had time to talk, and strongly
Disagree about the living out
Of life. There was no need to shout.
Rightly or else quite wrongly
We have run out of time, if not of talk.
Let us then cavalierly fork
Our ways, since we, and all unknown,
Have called into question one another's own.

The war horse

This dry night, nothing unusual
About the clip, clop, casual

Iron of his shoes as he stamps death
Like a mint on the innocent coinage of earth.

I lift the window, watch the ambling feather
Of hock and fetlock, loosed from its daily tether

In the tinker camp on the Enniskerry Road,
Pass, his breath hissing, his snuffling head

Down. He is gone. No great harm is done.
Only a leaf of our laurel hedge is torn

Of distant interest like a maimed limb,
Only a rose which now will never climb

The stone of our house, expendable, a mere
Line of defence against him, a volunteer

You might say, only a crocus its bulbous head
Blown from growth, one of the screamless dead.

But we, we are safe, our unformed fear
Of fierce commitment gone; why should we care

If a rose, a hedge, a crocus are uprooted
Like corpses, remote, crushed, mutilated?

He stumbles on like a rumour of war, huge,
Threatening; neighbours use the subterfuge

Of curtains; he stumbles down our short street
Thankfully passing us. I pause, wait,

Then to breathe relief lean on the sill
And for a second only my blood is still

With atavism. That rose he smashed frays
Ribboned across our hedge, recalling days

Of burned countryside, illicit braid:
A cause ruined before, a world betrayed.

Child of our time

for Aengus

Yesterday I knew no lullaby
But you have taught me overnight to order
This song, which takes from your final cry
Its tune, from your unreasoned end its reason;
Its rhythm from the discord of your murder
Its motive from the fact you cannot listen.

We who should have known how to instruct
With rhymes for your waking, rhythms for your sleep,
Names for the animals you took to bed,
Tales to distract, legends to protect,
Later an idiom for you to keep
And living, learn, must learn from you, dead,

To make our broken images rebuild
Themselves around your limbs, your broken
Image, find for your sake whose life our idle
Talk has cost, a new language. Child
Of our time, our times have robbed your cradle.
Sleep in a world your final sleep has woken.

17 May 1974

Conversation with an Inspector of Taxes

after Mayakovsky

No, Comrade Inspector, I won't sit down,
Thank you; forgive me taxing your time.
What a delicate matter this business of mine
Is, the more difficult since I am
Concerned to discern the role of the poet
Within the ranks of the proletariat.

If you knew how you've added to my troubles
Taxing me like a shopkeeper or kulak –
For six months you claim five hundred roubles
And twenty-five for the forms I didn't send back.
Yet I work the same as any, look what I've lost
In production and what my materials cost.

Perhaps I should explain it in your idiom:
What you call a promissory note
Is roughly the equivalent of rhyme
To us, owed to each and every alternate
Line while in the petty cash of sense
We moisten the coins of nuance.

Suppose I select a word to go
Into a line, it won't fit, I start
To force it and the next thing I know
The seams of the stanza strain apart.
Comrade Inspector, I can give
Assurance that words come expensive.

To revert now to poetic licence:
Metaphorically speaking my rhyming
Is a keg of dynamite, my lines
Smoulder towards it slowly, the timing
Device detonates and finally
The whole poem blows sky high.

Accusing me from your questionnaire
I see, 'Have you travelled in the course
Of business?' What if every year
I've bitted and stampeded Pegasus
Till both of us were worn? Have some sense.
Take into account the following instance.

There may be in Venezuela five
Or six pristine rhymes undiscovered.
If in pursuit of them I have
Tax to pay on travel, then my fevered
Search would draw too mean a loan
For poetry to sack the unknown.

Considering all this will you allow
Me a small mercenary reprieve?
I'll accept an inch of clay, a plough;
I'll be a peasant. Otherwise I achieve
So little by this speech that its effect,
Nil on you, on me I expect,

Will be years from now, I am sure,
These lines like ones in a puppet show,
Will jerk you back, inking your signature
On final demands and so, Comrade, so
I will have guaranteed your encore
Years after I have died and lie a pauper,

Crushed not by you bureaucrat
Though your claims are irritating, true,
But by the vast claims on a poet
I could not meet. All my debts to you
Are those of any chance financial sinner
But those to follow are my debts of honour:

To the Red Army, boiling across frontiers
In a wash of Cossack stallions, coats
Threaded from goat hide, unshaved hairs
Masking them like bandits, their supporters
Cheering them as the musket shots
Ventilate each of their deserters:

To the winter flowering cherry of Japan,
Frail as a foundling which never found
In my verse even the shelter given
To it by the snows which surround
Its blossom stealthily like rags heaped
Over a sprawled vagrant where he slept:

Finally I know myself indebted
Beyond anything I can return
To the fastness of my winter cradle
Because somehow I never celebrated
Its bleak skies; to this day they remain
Unsung while my tongue is idle.

Solitary

Night:
An oratory of dark,
a chapel of unreason.

Here in the shrubbery
the shrine.
I am its votary,
its season.

Flames
single
to my fingers

expert
to pick out
their heart,
the sacred heat

none may violate.
You could die for this.
The gods could make you blind.

I defy them.
I know,
only I know

these incendiary
and frenzied ways:
I am alone

no one's here,
no one sees
my hands

fan and cup,
my thumbs tinder.
How it leaps

from spark to blaze!
I flush
I darken.

How my flesh summers,
how my mind shadows
meshed in this brightness

how my cry
blasphemes
light and dark,
screams
land from sea,
makes word flesh
that now makes me

21

animal,
inanimate,
satiate,

and back I go
to a slack tip,
a light.

I stint my worship,
the cold watch I keep.
Fires flint somewhere else.
I winter
into sleep.

A ballad of beauty and time

Plainly came the time
The eucalyptus tree
Could not succour me,
Nor the honey-pot,
The sunshine vitamin,
Nor even getting thin:
I had passed my prime.

Then when bagged ash,
Scalded quarts of water,
Oil of the lime,
Cinders for the skin
And honey all had failed
I sorted out my money
And went to buy some time.

I knew the right address,
The occult house of shame
Where all the women came
Shopping for a mouth,
A new nose, an eyebrow
And entered without knocking
And stood as I did now.

A shape with a knife
Stooped away from me
Cutting something vague.
It might have been a face.
I couldn't really see.
I coughed once and said
'I want a lease of life'.

The room was full of masks,
Lines of grins gaping,
A wall of skin stretching,
A chin he had re-worked,
A face he had re-made.
He slit and cut and tucked
Then straightened from his blade.

'A tuck, a hem' he said –
'I only seam the line.
I only mend the dress.
It wouldn't do for you.
Your quarrel's with the weave.
The best I achieve
Is just a stitch in time.'

I started out again.
I knew a studio
Strewn with cold heels,
Closed in marble shock.
I saw the sculptor there
Chiselling a nose
And button-holed his smock:

'It's all very well
When you have bronzed a woman,
Pinioned her and finned
Wings on either shoulder.
Anyone can see
She won't get any older.
What good is that to me?

'See the last of youth
Slumming in my skin,
My sham pink mouth.
Here behold your critic –
The threat to your aesthetic.
I am the brute proof
Beauty is not truth.'

'Truth is in our lies'
He angrily replied:
'This woman fledged in stone
The centre of all eyes,
Her own museum-blind.
We sharpen with our skills
The arts of compromise.'

'And all I have cast
In crystal or in glass,
In lapis or in onyx
Is from my knowledge of
When from the honest flaw
To lift and stay my hand
And say "let it stand".'

RICHARD RYAN

Richard Ryan was born in 1946 and educated
at University College, Dublin, where he
taught in the English Department during
1972 and 1973. He then joined the Irish
Foreign Service and is presently attached to
the Permanent Irish Delegation at Brusssels.

Publications:
Ledges, Dolmen, 1970
Ravenswood, Dolmen, 1973

Father of famine

for Liam O'Flaherty

Shadow boxer, fighting
Man, old locust
Eater, bruised waxwing
Of the nest of dust;
O feeder of honey to the dead –
Mon père,
I would be led:
Must I neglect food to know hunger?

Famine village

This maze of stones which the wind cuts and hones
Smooth now, was in another century
The houses of famine fishermen, where bones

Long scattered, now without a memory,
Have fertilised this bramble wilderness
Of grass and thistle reaching to the knee,

Which press upward and thicken, and caress
The naked chimneys and the broken walls
Breathing the sea-mist and the emptiness.

Where once children played, now only gulls' calls
Echo and die slowly across the wide
Wild curve of sand to where the mountain falls

Into the sea. From the sick land they tried
To work the tide; they lived a life-long fight
To live and lost to graves on Slieve More's side.

Now a grey rain thickens the fading light.
Slowly the ruins become the mist and
Merge silently with the descending night.

Knockmany

for John Montague

In slow procession
trees ascend
the hill, enter
the mist-held ring
to crowd, chanting,
around the silent
hive of stones.

Giant tree-priests,
slowly they rock
in prayer; searching
the earth long root
veins writhe down-
ward, probing
for blood the deep

hill's heart. As
the quick sap stirs,
runnels upward
through trunk and
thigh, filling
with its white life
the glistening loins,

louder the branches,
bone-hard arms
dipping, digging
up air, moan –
mad with certainty –
as the mist,
prised up like a stone,

reveals a monstrous
shadow rising, rising
through the forked, skinless
fingers – the swaying trees
lean forward now, humming,
to clutch and lift
their twitching burden.

Winter in Minneapolis

for Eóin McKiernan

From my high window I can watch
the freeways coiling on their strange
stilts to where the city glows
through rain like a new planet.

Tonight the radio speaks
of snow and in the waste plots
below trees stiffen,
frost wrinkles the pools.

Through high dark air
the apartment buildings,
like computer panels, begin
again to transmit their faint signals –

for they are there now, freed one and all
from the far windy towns, the thin
bright girls compounded of heat,
movement, and a few portable needs.

But I have no calls to make tonight,
for we are all strangers here
who have only the night to share –
stereos, soft lights, and small alarm clocks:

of our photograph albums, our far
towns, and our silences we do not speak;
wisely we have learned to respect
the locked door and unanswered telephone.

I turn from my window and pause a moment
in darkness. My bed and desk
barely visible, clean paper
waits in its neat circle of light. . .

I wait; and slowly they appear, singly,
like apparitions. They stand all round me,
on metal bridges and in the wet streets,
their long hair blowing and they will not go.

From My Lai the thunder went west

and it all died down
to an underground
tapping and then that,
too, stopped dead.

In cornfield, wheat
field, a black
sheet of earth
was drawn neatly

across the seed
they planted.
And the fields turn
daily to the sun.

Come high Summer
and the first shoots
will appear, puzzling
the sun as, growing

through earth, growing
through grass, the
human crop they have sown –
child bone, wife

bone, man
bone will stand
wavering in the pale fields:
the silent, eye-

less army will
march west through
Autumn and Europe
until, streaked

with December rain
they will stand in
New York and Texas;
as the lights click

out across America
they will fence in
the houses, tapping
on window, tapping

on door. Till
dawn, then rain only:
from sea to sea drifting,
drops of bright ruby.

God the Father

I will not travel tonight.
Toward dawn a star
In Andromeda will abruptly

Die but the world and his wife,
Tonight carefully shrouded in snow
Where they live, will see

Nothing of it and instead may marvel
With drinks through glass
At a slow lace of snow slipping

Down the darkening limbs of trees
Only or, if that bores them,
May number as they drift together

Toward sleep the thin
Skins of heat like leaves
Slipping from little hands

And little feet, feeling
Their warm houses with leaves
And snow filling, the children's rooms

Softly into dark drifts
Tilting, may if they can at dawn
Take such comfort as they might need

From the high spars
of trees returning safely
Home on a grey tide and,

Under the trees, a few
Calm stars straying down
Over the rim of the planet

Of the living where each brain
In its pit stirs again
For me only, a world

Recollects its purpose
And abroad I go once more,
Savouring my choices

As there – and there – life
Whistles from a clutch of thorn,
Spawns bone in the humming ponds.

MICHAEL FOLEY

Michael Foley was born in Derry in 1947. He is currently working in Dublin as a Computer Science Lecturer.

Publications:
True Life Love Stories, Blackstaff Press, 1976
The Irish Frog, imitations from French poetry, Ulsterman Publications, 1978
The Life of Jamesie Coyle, novel serialised in *Fortnight* magazine, 1977
The GO Situation, Blackstaff Press, 1982

from True Life Love Stories

1
Great fleshy upper arms with
    vaccination marks.
Lime green and knock-your-eye-out pink.
    Soiled white bra straps.

They hand you their lighters and
    twenties of cigs. You
dance, one hand on flesh, the other
    light on faintly creaking

corsetage. Wild theories crowd your brain –
    anaemic cool conceals
tremendous heat – one touch and milk-
    white thighs will part like

well-cooked meat. Once round, such faintness floods
    your throbbing voyeur soul!
You reel and swoon – completely zonked
    provincial Baudelaire!

21
No comrades in the old sense now
    no young boy net-
work moving in with booze and
    gritty jokes. There's

times I wouldn't mind a touch of
    that – but we won't
shirk our fate, the dreadful towns, the
    sordid need to work.

Let's see if the breeding will out.
    'I'm sure this thing can still
be done with style – each night a murmur
    A demain, mon cher

sweet manners in a sordid world,
      spry grin and (slightly
tatty) monkey suit – the panic, like
      the stomach, well held in.

23
The blossoms are coming adrift
      by the easter gate.
Aiee! It is time. My name will be
      forgotten here. I go

to the east, to a job. I'm almost
      sure this choice is right.
My mistress calls from the north room
      Make ready, all's prepared

We are going to seek the
      anonymous life.
For it seems to me now like
      the trick is to live

like a clerk but not be a clerk.
      Inspire me, mistress
of the unbound hair. So many
      really are straight clerks.

24
I'm scared to go away, cherie.
      I've been before
but with chaps. They *are* a help. They
      appreciate irony,

when helpless there's helpless laughter
      at least. Your conduct is
satisfactory, yes – but never yet
      tested under stress.

Might it pop like a broken bulb?
    (Where was Foley
when the light went out?) Ah how shall
    we manage at all?

Who'll love our twisted Papish hearts?
    Who'll be our friends
in the time to come?. . . And think of the
    letters we'll have to write!

25
Our great ship swings around in the mist
    and points, if not at
poverty, at least at something tough.
    Where will this course end?

Will I go round the bend and drag
    leftluggagewards
her dripping head in a box? Or
    will there be merely

silence, she asleep, I noting
    ruined squaw hands?
Who'll know we've been heroic if
    we merely disappear?

Who'll tell the tale? Who'll protest the
    unnecessary
squalor and work – *that wasn't germane
    Mister Chairman Sir?*

I remember Adlestrop

Yes, I remember Adlestrop.
Such an innocent vague
Neither-here-nor-there poem
– Yet it started so much crap.

Though Thomas was no rat
His poem began the trend
This impression of *Big Things* going on
Though of course you're not told what.

And that resonant hum in the air
As the frigid final phrase
Falls into its well-judged place.
By God, you think, *there's something there.*

All the vaguely mysterious
Bogusly sonorous
Phoneyly resonant slop!
Oh I remember Adlestrop.

Through the gateless gate

The invitations falling off,
my 'contacts' dying out.
And it's not bad luck – it's sloth.
I'm happy to flop at the 'talented' life.
(My mentors give up in disgust.)

I wanted it all but was stingy with time,
too loath to leave the common round.

Amazing but the truth!
To find it in the common round,
borne through the gateless gate at last,
away on the soul's authentic quest!

And I with a foot on the bottom rung,
one of 'Ten Irish Poets' last year!

Poor people in church

Nobody loves the lugubrious slave
(The seaside donkey is always kicked)
Here placid work beasts trained to behave
Crawl to have their old wounds licked.

All eyes on the chancel dripping gold
And sniffing the odour of wax like bread
Their ridiculous stubborn prayers unfold
Prayers of thanksgiving, prayers of dread.

Bella Doherty, after her ninth warned more
Would mean certain death but left alone
In a ward with her man, was tested before
She got out and found pregnant again.

Lily Sweeny's boy hated his job. Lily prayed,
That factory only a curse to the town
Her confidence in him fully repaid
When Blessed Martin closed it down.

Though wearing these benches smooth is sane enough
Apart from any favours saints may grant
When they've drunk men who cut up rough
And think a good slap's what they really want.

And tonight preparations go on, a rare bonus
Of bustle and noise which they watch in awe, so proud
Of next week's televised Midnight Mass
(No coughers or wheezers allowed).

Their new bishop, youngest in Ireland, fixed
It, prized for his flair and drive in raising funds
(Ex-Bingo King) and for his readiness to mix
(Always snapped pumping flesh in the slums).

But now, awesomely assured and overdressed,
Freezing the poor – Sweet Christ! – in their seats
With the jaundiced glare of their class, unimpressed
It's the ladies from swankier streets.

Observing the pious frowns, the bags and hats
You wouldn't believe the schemes of this bunch
Disputing the coveted four hundred seats
For the Bishop's Inauguration Buffet Lunch!

Corbière's eternal feminine

On our backs you crack the whip of your caprice
Allowing us pleasures vivid but fleeting
Before the swift permanent fall from grace
To insomnia, booze and compulsive eating

Raiding the late-night delicatessen
For cream cakes and Black Forest gateau
– Though the sorrow and pain don't lessen
As the black night wears on, long and slow.

Bitch curled up foetus-wise
Fitting against your stud with sighs
May you learn what it's like to weep

With clenched teeth in impotent fury
Mouth tasting of horse-blanket puree
Even tossing off bringing no sleep.

HUGH MAXTON

Hugh Maxton was born in Wicklow, in 1947,
and educated at Trinity College, Dublin.
From 1971 to 1974 he lived in Derry before
he moved to Yorkshire. He lectures at the
University of Leeds.

Publications:
Stones, Allen Figgis, 1970
The Noise of the Fields, Dolmen, 1976

Critical works:
Sheridan Le Fanu and Victorian Ireland,
Oxford University Press, 1980

Premonition of winter

We have come to love this coastline. Clearly
the cobbles here are looser than in town
and the dust is crystalline. We nearly
think another world begins or, grown
casual, imagine seas and channels
separate us from the work-a-day mass.

But these rocks are the more ancient hells,
the acid coves and strands of powdered glass.
In Antrim sheep were bled dry by a beast
not known to man but intimate with glands
and arteries. A whale skidded at least
twelve yards ashore against the rush of land.

In the town they talk of peace and justice
but have never known the sea turn to ice.

Risk

i. m. Máirtín Ó Cadhain

When you chaired a meeting in Trinity
you refused to open until the man
from the Special Branch had left the back row.
You sat there reading while the audience
hoped you weren't making a fool of yourself.
At last someone deserted out of loyalty.

We never saw you as a widower
vainly stocking a life with whiskey,
nor saw the massive verso timetables
which you wrote those last stories on, nor heard
your shy inquiries about drainage maps.
The Sheaves are Stacked; your shade is lightening now.

At the funeral you scored a final point,
refusing to hear a volley of shots.

Ode

To read our few poets
you'd think there had been
a recent withdrawal
from the land of the stoat
and the yellow-scarf mouse;

a land in which nothing
twitches in the woodlands
but our nerves,
and every swan
is someone else's daughter.

Their lives are mashed
in the engine of politics
or, high on dynamite,
they industrialise the old dreads.
Yet truth is

ours is still a rural country.
In which we never need
the stoat for savagery
or the yellow-scarf
for extinction.

from Elegies

1

When John Donne dropped to sleep all around him slept.
Pictures were drowsy on the wall, the floor
was deep in rugs and tables; furniture
whose certain essence was a sleep that kept
the clocks as motionless as lumber.
At rest in cupboards as in dormitories
the linen slept as though it were bodies
draped in animal slumber.
Night was not idly here and there
turning the key or coiled in locks
but paused in heat exhaling human shocks
to be at once impenetrable as air.
All slept: the window in its envelope
of snow might never have been written;
the words it might have read remained unseen
when John Donne awakened and took his sleep.

The iron weights in the butcher's shop are prone
in care of watchdogs shrunken from the chains.
Mice are asleep and cats stiffened; the Thames
nods its way towards a salted dawn
shaking the reflected tower and arch.
Ships are anchorless by the wharf safely.
The sea lies down beside a promontory,
the land her bolster, intent and white as starch.
The walls of the gaol loosen in this rest
and prisoners lie still in their freedom
heedless of a momentary calm
before light draws its finger from the east.

The angels also sleep above the globe,
a world forgotten by the sleeping saints.
In holy shame fair paradise faints
under the waves of the Lord's deepest robe.

Gehenna sleeps and man must fail to be;
John Donne fails tonight his last disaster;
his breath and kiss and manly lines are lost.
Satan sleeps, and with him all enmity.
The prophets sleep. Good rests on Evil's arm.
The paling snow completes its last full stop
as his stressed and weary syllables drop
in place, to his drift of words' alarm.
Everybody sleeps: the saints, devils, God,
friends, deceitful servants, lovers in bed
lie dormant on this night John Donne is dead.
And the snow shuffles its feet on the road.

PAUL MURRAY

Paul Murray was born in 1947 in Newcastle,
Co. Down. Educated at St Malachy's College,
Belfast, he entered the Dominican Order in
1966 and is at present assigned to St Mary's,
Tallaght, Co. Dublin.

Publications:
Ritual Poems, New Writers Press, 1971
Rites and Meditations, Dolmen, 1982

Critical works:
The Mysticism Debate (a brief study of
mysticism), Chicago, 1978

Possessed

Whose name is Legion speak.

Was it a shadow merely sang
Under him the stroke
Of burning seed;

Who fathered him his sight: was
It the phoenix bird winged
Giddy over flame?

Who have possessed him, answer:

How in the empty socket of his eyes
Appeared the brilliant sun,
Twice over.

Death of a priest

Only afterwards, when flesh succumbed
And he could feel his last
Breath freeze against her cheek,
And somewhere in the distance, chorus
Contra chorum, could hear
The De Profundis plead for him,
Was he afraid.

A black breviary propped between his
Chest and chin, a cold
Hand closing his eyes, touching
Without chrism his wrinkled forehead;
Only then could he believe
She was neither fantasy of daydream
Nor temptation: Death.

A kind of palmistry

We were not superstitious; this medium
was simply our first way through
to each other:

You, telling my fortune and I, feeling
your small hot palm
make love to my fingers.

It was little more than friendship;
though once, appearing
to take my adolescent life-line

Seriously, you spelt out unmistakable
meaning, auspiciously
suggestive at the time; and yet,

By virtue of my conscience intervening,
never was so favourable an omen
less prophetic.

Introit

This morning,
on entering the cold chapel,

       I looked first
to the sun, as the pagan does;
not by strict custom
nor by constraint, but because

I too, as creature,
sense man's primitive emotion:
his need to praise.
And so, like priest or pagan,

according
as the sun moves, I perform
this ancient ritual.
And though not always able

to approach,
often, effaced in light, I stand
before this
chalice of the morning,

I break this
ordinary bread as something holy.

FRANK ORMSBY

Frank Ormsby was born in Enniskillen,
Co. Fermanagh, in 1947 and educated at
St Michael's College, and Queen's University,
Belfast. He is editor of *The Honest Ulsterman*
and teaches English at The Royal Belfast
Academical Institution. He won a Gregory
Award in 1974.

Publications:
A Store of Candles,
Oxford University Press, 1977

As editor:
Poets from the North of Ireland,
Blackstaff Press, 1979

Landscape with figures

What haunts me is a farmhouse among trees
Seen from a bus window, a girl
With a suitcase climbing a long hill
And a woman waiting.
The time the bus took to reach and pass
The lane's entrance nothing was settled,
The girl still climbing and the woman still
On the long hill's summit.

Men were not present. Neither in the fields
That sloped from hedges, nor beyond the wall
That marked the yard's limits
Was there sign of hens, or hands working.
No sight that might have softened
On the eye the scene's
Relentlessness.

Nothing had happened, yet the minute spoke
And the scene spoke and the silence,
And oppressed as air does, loading
For a storm's release.

All lanes and houses
Secretive in trees and gaunt hills' jawlines
Turn my thoughts again
To that day's journey and the thing I saw
And could not fathom. Struck with the same dread
I seem to share in sense, not detail,
What was heavy there:
Sadness of dim places, obscure lives,
Ends and beginnings,
Such extremities.

After Mass

It's Sunday and the country boys have come
To woo from a distance. Intent, they loiter.
One has re-oiled his bicycle, another
Washed his underpants in the Slane river.

The bridge she sits on is of crumbling stone
And slopes in the water. Swinging her legs
She seems indifferent; intent is all they manage.
Fixed where they are they nudge and scratch and mutter:

'The thatch is on, the tenant should be in.'

Sheepman

Even the barflies move to corner tables,
Mouthing 'Sheepman'. The barman serves,
But grudgingly. Like Mexicans and half-
Breeds I must wear that special hangdog look,
Say nothing.

There is too much cattle country. The range
Is free in theory, cowmen find
Excuses to resent the different.
They claim that cows won't feed where sheep have fed.
Pathetic.

Don't say the outcast has his dignity.
Perhaps it's something not to thrive
On brawn, or trample those whose small stampedes
Hurt no one; such victories are thin, cold
Consolation.

Unbowed I claim my rights – to herd alone,
And be accepted. When I skirt
The rim of cattle drives, salute me,
And when I come to share your bunkhouse fire,
Make room.

The edge of war

The edge of war in a provincial town
Before I was born: the quarries prospered,
Blasting out the stones to build an airfield.
Camps were constructed, training grounds deployed
In sheltered woodland.

Such headline moments! Eisenhower on tour
And local planes sighting the *Bismarck;*
A Wings-for-Victory Week, mobile canteens.
War was a bracing current in the streams
Of a small county.

And once, in the hours of a sombre dawn,
A crowd at the station. Their faces to
Belfast, haunted by a glow that hung on
The skyline, seemed no more to know the edge
Of local quarrels. In their arms thick

Blankets for the refugees.

Under the stairs

Look in the dark alcove under the stairs:
a paintbrush steeped in turpentine, its hairs

softening for use; rat-poison in a jar;
bent spoons for prising lids; a spare fire-bar;

the shaft of a broom; a tyre; assorted nails;
a store of candles for when the light fails.

Floods

At high tide the sea is under the city,
A natural subversive. The Farset,
Forced underground, observes no curfew,
And, sleepless in their beds, the sullen drains
Move under manholes.

Blame fall on the builders, foolish men.
This strained civility of city, sea, breaks
Yearly, snapped by native rains,
Leaving in low streets and sandbagged doors,
The furnished pavements.

Islands

The week Makarios fell we moved house.
His crisis was not ours or near home.
Caught from the hall those bulletins defined
Less than heaped chairs the time's upheaval.

The Turks invaded. Half-way up a wall
With hammer, nails, my focus of concern
Was hanging pictures. Above the city
Bloomed no paratroops. The streets were empty.

And years from now when people ask how long
We've lived here, we will need no calendars.
A voice, untroubled, in the mind will tell:
We moved in the week Makarios fell.

Incurables

Plaques and a marble silence about the door
of the Ulster Cancer Foundation, the air a tissue
shredding between the chimneys and the moon.
We eavesdrop on police-cars, the shift and crackle
of ice in the wavelengths.
Our charts are frosty promises. Their troughs
may suck us down forever, and who will know
or care what perished.
Or children may have the peace
to say of us: 'They lived in troubled times.
They stayed afloat and somehow kept their warmth.'
For now, we are grateful that our breath still wreathes
east of the City Cemetery, stainless skies
between us and the troubled distances.
The blinds are lit, the moon is finding gold
in every street's mouthful of worn cobbles.

Survivors

Sometimes they cross an avenue at dusk,
those hoarse-voiced children brashly on the move
from mews to alley. Mostly they seem too young
to keep such hours and underdressed for air
that cuts its teeth on glass and barbed-wire coils,
the rusted nails of half-wrecked garages.
They root behind our lives for what they can find:
the bones of broken telephones, old cars
picked bare already to their oiliest springs,
dead spars along the embankment. They hug their loads
of chosen bric-a-brac and, blindly assured,
ignite with purposes: to float an ark
or point a bonfire, angle a sheet of tin
against a brick coalhouse and call it home
or call it a tree-house. As they flit from view
their voices sack the twilight. They seem to cry:
'We're tougher than you think, friend, tough as old boots.
You haven't seen the last of us. Goodbye.'

King William Park

The mountains must have watched it, the startled eyes
of swamp-life and the long-shinned estuary birds:
that tidal glitter curling out to sea
for the last time, abandoning its mud.
Then centuries of minute adjustments, rivers
changing their beds,
the shifting work of sloblands under the sky
and fibrous growths toughening, holding their own.

Fowlers, fishers and settlers, intricate drains,
channels and cargoes, chimneys, streetlamps and trams;
but always the brickwork tilting, buildings on stilts,
the tide-swell echoes creeping out of the ground
yearly to meet the rainfall and shaping themselves
to crests and troughs in the tarmac, undulant cobbles.
Or pouring their excess out of sudden wounds
in streets miles inland.

Here, where the park is, breakers found a shore
to bury shells, jetsam a place to lie.
Daily the winos spend their bleary rage
in squabbles among the benches,
or sing their hearts out searching for a song
on a green patch with trees beside a junction.
And knee-capped boys on crutches raise their heads
to follow us past the railings,

wintry eyes asking how far we have come
and where we are going. A terraced marsh away
sludge-pumps have sucked a resting-place for stone;
the blocks of a new hospital are hauled
through scaffolding, past windows where the sun
flames in the evening gloriously, or the rain
drifts into soundless networks on its way
to the earth-clogged ears in the groundwork, the listening shells.

CIARAN CARSON

Ciarán Carson was born in 1948 in Belfast.
A graduate of Queen's University, he was a
teacher and Civil Servant for a time and is
now Traditional Arts Officer
with the Arts Council. He won an Eric
Gregory Award in 1978.

Publications:
The New Estate, Blackstaff Press, 1976

The Half-Moon Lake

It was here the boy entered the skylight
And was gone, into the reversed world
Of his dreams, hoping that life there might

Prove otherwise. Walking the tentative
Pane of ice there might have been that morning,
He would have imagined himself to live

In one final image, the star-shaped hole
Approaching darkly, sudden as his
Disappearance from our lives. Or had his soul

Just then been frailed too taut
For human heart, had the white sheet
Already failed beneath him at the thought?

No one heard him go in silence,
Nor when they dragged for him, deep as chance
Allowed, was there any trace.

Was the faultless mirror shattered
By the thin boy diving for the moon
Of his own face rising through the water?

They could not yet say why
He left so quickly, not leaving any word,
Or whether the glass existed purely

For his own forgetfulness. Deep
In the unseen water it is possible
He lies, with himself at last asleep.

It was for the other children that they feared.
It had been necessary that the Half-Moon Lake be
Filled in, and altogether disappear.

O'Carolan's complaint

The great tunes
I never played are lost
To monied patronage, the lit rooms
In grey façades

Whisper, fall silent
At their harmony and grace. I think
Of all the girls I might have loved
Instead of music –

One hand finding melody
As easily as the pulse of a heart,
The other making fluent gestures
Towards the purse of love.

My real performances
Never yet embraced an actual beauty –
Mere competence, my inward ear
And theirs heard better:

Like intervals of silence
Between the notes,
Their upturned faces wanting more,
The lives I never lived.

The bomb disposal

Is it just like picking a lock
with the slow deliberation of a funeral,
hesitating through a darkened nave
until you find the answer?

Listening to the malevolent tick
of its heart, can you read
the message of the threaded veins
like print, its body's chart?

The city is a map of the city,
its forbidden areas changing daily.
I find myself in a crowded taxi
making deviations from the known route,

ending in a cul-de-sac
where everyone breaks out suddenly
in whispers, noting the boarded windows,
the drawn blinds.

Linen

From the photographs of bleach-greens
Mill-hands stare across the snowy acres.
In a frieze white as marble
Their lives are ravelled and unravelled –
Golden straw, bright thread, the iron looms
Are cast in tangled cordage.

The shapes of wheels and spindles shine
In darkness. When the weave is finished,
Light will fall on linen simply, as it would
On glass, or silverware, or water,
Things needed for a wedding or a funeral;
We will be reconciled to those cold sheets.

Our country cousins

On birthdays
or your goings-away

to become black sheep
we'd sleep

in each other's
houses then, mothers

being sisters again,
lying apart from their men;

dressed in clothes of another kind,
we'd play blind

man's buff,
the farmer wants a wife,

knowing our real kin
to lie beneath the skin.

Our ones
would be buried with your ones.

Someone, pretending an accident,
wore bandages, sent

his partner with a knife in her head.
Another painted his body red.

Even your eggs were flecked with blood,
your bread had the coarse grain of tweed.

Visitors

The clock tinkles; a silver needle
moves. Aunt Rose nods and waves in the bowed glass
of the china cabinet, a glint of gold rims
as she fills a cup. I touch the curved wrist
of her walking stick, though I am not allowed.
I sprinkle sugar on my bread and butter.

Now she is shown photographs of me
decreasing like the thin smile of the dogs
perched on the mantelpiece.
I am wearing a new blazer on my first day
at school. I am already walking. Now I am
in the cradle. You cannot see my face.

I will escape to the kitchen larder
and inhale the treacle depths, the snuff of cloves
and cinnamon. I am already half-asleep again,
thinking how my fingers will not close.
They poke through the slats of the air-grille.
A light breeze comes from nowhere.

East of Cairo

One day I walked into the village compound
and found the headsman and his family watching television.
They were sitting in rickety bamboo chairs
and it was pouring rain, but no one seemed to mind.

It was one of those travelogues on French Cambodia.
A policeman was directing traffic. Temples,
cows and awnings rippled in the sun. Maidens danced
around with bangles on their arms. The usual stuff.

Why did these people sit here, watching this?
Could they not be themselves? It was then I decided
to leave Sarajasthan. I had come to the East, after all,
to find myself, and there was nothing there.

I now have plans to go to the holy city of Lhasa.
They say the only wheel there is a prayer-wheel.
And I hear that the Dalai Lama has a scheme
to separate the spirit from the body.

All day long, from high in his palace tower,
the god-king stares through Swiss binoculars
at three monks gliding on the river
on ice-skates left them by the last explorer.

Smithfield

I have forgotten something, I am
going back. The wrought iron flowers
of the gate breathe open to
sooty alcoves, the withered shelves
of books. There is a light
that glints off tin and earthenware
reminding me of touch, the beaded moulding
of a picture-frame –

here is a hand that beckons from
an empty doorway. Open the gilt clasp,
the book of strangers:
the families arranged with roses,
the brothers, the sister
in her First Communion frock, their hands
like ornaments in mine beneath
the muffled ribs of gloves:

we are all walking to school
past the face of a clock, linked
together in the glass dark of the
undertaker's window: one, two, three, four
figures in the gilt lettering.
Soon it will be dusk, and all of us are sent
to find each other, though each
of us is lost in a separate field:

over the waving meadow, through
the trees, a gap of light sways
like a face, a hand discovering itself
among the branches and the inlets.
One of us has fallen in the river;
the stream of my mother's veil at the porch,
sunlight on a brick wall smiling
with the child who is not there.

TOM PAULIN

Tom Paulin was born in Leeds in 1949 and
grew up in Belfast. Educated at Hull and
Oxford Universities, he now lectures in
English at the University of Nottingham. He
received a Gregory Award in 1976 and the
Somerset Maugham Award in 1978.

Publications:
A State of Justice, Faber, 1977
The Strange Museum, Faber, 1980

Critical works:
The Poetry of Perception (on
Thomas Hardy), Gill and Macmillan, 1975

A September rising

I nearly saw them this morning.
There was rust in the beech leaves,
The branches were twisted and nude, grey
In the glistening from a blue that stretched
The subtlest, the finest of frosts.

They were there in that air,
Faintly cheeping, chittering a white
Web in the blue. Changing and staying still.
Squaddies and navvies perhaps, but
Mainly the spirit grocers.

Beyond politeness, justified;
Beyond salt bacon and rickety bells
Jangled on light doors by their betters.
The invisible purveyors of provisions,
Glad now in their fine element.

They could chicker above the trees
In the blue air, they could be
Queerly happy and seethe like sprats,
Like fresh silver in the deepest drawer.
Everywhere their names are fading.

They are taken down, stranded
Among speed, on forgotten shelves
In the back offices of new democracies;
But they live, they live again
Above brick cities which are soldiers' villages.

In Antrim

Her son is sick and she clears it up.
In twenty years, though he smiles,
He's spoken
Maybe ten different words to her.

The lough's dying, the road's empty.
Near a derelict, Twenties bungalow
I watch them from a distance –
Mother, brother.

Young funerals

A nameless visual.
A series of walls, covered windows,
Doors opening into the shared street.
The terrace brings out its dead.

The girl's small coffin, a new glossiness,
Moving through a windy afternoon.

Two doors down, the boy is dying
In his bedroom. It takes months.

When the thin blinds are drawn
I'll hurry past on the other side.
They must not touch me, these deaths.

His parents are names, a different number.
The front room is photographs and wept shadows,
An empty shop that gives away misery.

Bradley the last idealist

For some reason he never actually taught
Anyone; said a nervous complication
Prevented him, which was why his scout brought
Him over to Savoy each long vacation.
There, every morning on his own, he caught
A cable-car up into the mountains
Where he convalesced on beds of gentians.

Surrounded by blue sky and clouds, he lay
Intently staring into the far distance,
His rapt mind transfixed on Mont Blanc all day
Until absolutely locked in a deep white trance.
He left everything behind him then – the clay,
The cats, books, gowns, nodding domes and misty spires,
Those vulgar details and those Cretan liars.

At nights in term, obscured from gentlemen and God,
He clipped a torch to his air-gun, put his hat
On and prowled stealthily around the dark quad
For cats, his aim utterly accurate –
An absolute guaranteed by torch and tripod.
Then, relishing those brief feline terrors,
He would squeeze gently into their green mirrors.

Still century

The hard captains of industry
Held the province in a firm control.

Judges, your pious tyranny
Is baked bone-dry in the old

Bricks of a hundred linen mills,
The shadows of black tabernacles.

A crowd moves along the Shankill,
And lamps shine in the dull

Streets where a fierce religion
Prays to the names of power:

Ewart and Bryson, Craig and Carson.
On every wall, texts or a thick char.

Stacked in the corners of factory-yards,
The wicker carboys of green acid

Hold out their bitter promise of whiteness
To the bleachgreens above the city.

The orange smoke at sunset, the gruff
Accents of a thousand foremen, speak

To the chosen, saying they are the stuff
The visions, cutlery and Belleek

China are laid on. They are tied
To the shade of a bearded god,

Their dream of happiness is his smile
And his skilful way with the hardest rod.

Anastasia McLaughlin

Her father is sick. He dozes most afternoons.
The nurse makes tea then and scans *The Newsletter*.
She has little to say to his grey daughter
Whose name began a strangeness the years took over.
His trade was flax and yarns, he brought her name
With an ikon and *matrioshka* – gifts for his wife
Who died the year that Carson's statue was unveiled.

McLaughlin is dreaming of a sermon he once heard
From a righteous preacher in a wooden pulpit
Who frowned upon a sinful brotherhood and shouted
The Word of deserts and rainy places where the Just
Are stretched to do the work a hard God sent them for.
His text was taken from the land of Uz
Where men are upright and their farms are walled.

'Though we may make sand to melt in a furnace
And make a mirror of it, we are as shadows
Thrown by a weaver's shuttle: and though we hide ourselves
In desolate cities and in empty houses,
His anger will seek us out till we shall hear
The accent of the destroyer, the sly champing
Of moths busy with the linen in our chests.'

He wakes to a dull afternoon like any other –
The musty dampness of his study, the window panes
That flaw his view of the lawn and settled trees.
The logs in the grate have turned to a soft ash.
The dour gardener who cut them is smoking
In the warm greenhouse, wondering did his nephew
Break in the week before and thieve McLaughlin's silver?

Constables came to the Mill House with alsatians,
And the wet spring was filled with uniforms and statements.
When they found nothing, they suspected everyone.
Even the plain woman who served them tea.

71

'Father, I am the lost daughter whose name you stole.
Your visions slide across these walls: dry lavender,
Old memories of all that wronged us. I am unkind.'

He sees his son below the bruised Atlantic,
And on a summer's morning in Great Victoria Street
He talks with Thomas Ferguson outside the Iceworks.
He sees the north stretched out upon the mountains,
Its dream of fair weather rubbing a bloom on rinsed slates;
He watches the mills prosper and grow derelict,
As he starts his journey to the Finland Station.

Where Art is a midwife

In the third decade of March,
A Tuesday in the town of Z—

The censors are on day-release.
They must learn about literature.

There are things called ironies,
Also symbols, which carry meaning.

The types of ambiguity
Are as numerous as the enemies

Of the state. Formal and bourgeois,
Sonnets sing of the old order,

Its lost gardens where white ladies
Are served wine in the subtle shade.

This poem about a bear
Is not a poem about a bear.

It might be termed a satire
On a loyal friend. Do I need

To spell it out? Is it possible
That none of you can understand?

The garden of self-delight

In that garden to the south
the civil gods are ranged
like statues in a maze
of vines and bay leaves.

The fountain grows a dance
of dreaming surfaces –
none of my slow guesses
will tell how deep they are.

And the men who walk the paths
murmur and hold hands
for they are special friends
who like a fragrant verse.

The taut women pass them by,
virgins of the moon
drifting through the cool
evening in their gowns.

This is a playful place,
though I view it from a bruised
shore that is dark blue
and cold and rigorous.

How can I understand
these fine and gracious beings
who pass me by and sing
lightly to each other?

Saying art is for itself
and prays to mirrors in the sand,
its own mirrors of burnt sand
where the smooth forms look pure.

So tell me there's no law,
and all of life is like a wine
that settles and grows ripe
till it dances on the tongue.

PATRICK WILLIAMS

Patrick Williams was born in Co. Down in
1950 and educated at Trinity College, Dublin.
He worked in London and Canada before
returning to Co. Down where he now lives.

Publications:
Trails, Sidgwick & Jackson, 1981

Home

The first week back it looked like Toytown,
But once I'd done the twelve bars to renew
Dislike, indifference, amity, and friendship,
Checked along Main Street and found a quorum
Of wise virgins, decent working men,
Housewives jousting in the shopping lists,
Local toughs and mean-eyed drifters from
The Falls and Shankill, seen our new young curate
Sleeking by with one hand on the wheel,
Admired the patient mountains, praised the sea
And bought a copy of *The Mourne Observer*
('Row at dance. Accused had drink taken.'),
Things began to settle. I was home.
Not much has changed. On Sunday mornings here
I meet the same dark suits escorting hats,
Insects scattered from a lifted stone
At seventeen, though after England's grey
Church of the Economy . . . and now
Even these seem ready for a better
Christ, more practical, but necromancers,
Jokers with a twist of bitterness.
Everybody everywhere I've been
Limps a little, here they limp a lot,
But here the disability has something
In common with my own. I need this place
To sit, to pare the crutch down for a pen.

Rhapsody on Main Street

For the first time since anyone remembers
They've opened the town from one end to the other,
Right from the Donard Bar to the Anchor.
Yellow diggers and men roaring commands
Make more noise and worse than tourist summer,
This year we're cheated of the dead of winter
When even at midday the street is ghostly,
Maybe a disconsolate street cleaner,
A few diehard wives, two cops
Plodding, debating if July is better –
Boozed children with knives in the arcades –
Or this black wind and the one lonely
Offence a frozen dog-turd curled on the pavement.
Fortunately I enjoy holes in the ground
And here I can stand and stare at the town's innards,
At pipes spiriting waste and water –
A thousand shithouse doors shyly closing,
The sudden triumphant flush and Yesterday
Off to be subdued with fierce chemicals –
Sweet water from heaven and the mountains
Into the Silent Valley to our kitchens,
Dousing the burning throats of hungover
Chain-smokers cursing Sunday mornings.
Electricity runs there too
Faster than the water or excrement,
It needs an outlet for its excitement.
This earth is alive and seems friendly,
It seems used to people, to accept
The town on top, so many generations
Have told it something of the human condition.
It's not the heavy shroud of clay inland
But where we walk and send human roots.
One night last week I fell in a trench
And lay back looking at the moon,
Singing snatches of songs as they came.
A passing drunk called, 'Hey! Want a hand?'

'No thanks. I'm fine down here.'
It struck me I wouldn't mind being buried there,
Under the living street and its seasons,
All the voices of July thinning
Through September's casual strollers talking
To quick or faltering steps on a winter's night
And then April and the children running.
I wouldn't be able to see through the tarmacadam
But maybe the roots of the tree in the priest's garden
Would whisper some news of the latest fashions,
The fights on Saturday nights, whose grandson
Was holding hands with whose granddaughter . . .
If the tree died or they cut it down
I'd still be better off than up in Bryansford –
They hear nothing, or now and then
Women weeping, the low voices of men.
In fifty or a hundred years' time
They'd open the street again and find me grinning
Wider than ever living, when I walked
Among them, felt them near, too near, and frowned.

Lines

I hear the trouble came
Through '68 in protest marches,
Out of centuries' injustice
Tightening since Dermot brought
An unwelcome visitor
Whose bruised foot is stuck in the door,
Squirming now in dented armour,
Wanting to go home.
I'd go further back
For the itch we scratch
With swords or atom bombs –

So tangled and insane
We couldn't disengage or care
Why we clawed and swore.
We found some grubby formula
To walk away with honour
In disgrace, our jotters
Crumpled, full of freakish nudes,
Bad grammar, half-done sums.

A marriage

Though they found each other
Like an accident
And the child was harmed
Who had to crawl away,
Come back to bury them,
Forgive and be forgiven,
Still they lie together,
His ring on her finger.
In a perfect world
It could never happen:
Computers would have wept
At the proposition.
No one would be fucked up.
No one would be born.

In the dark

They told me God came to Pius
When Pius was worried about the world
And couldn't sleep. I saw that room,
Severe, high-ceilinged, fill with light,
Pius sitting up in the bed
As God stood on the marble floor,
Arms folded, heavily-built,
Rugged, old, grave, erect,
Nodding slowly as Pius spoke,
Answering in muted thunder.

Years later in love in bed
Under you, over you, all along you
Till there was nothing left to do
Only enter you, climbing with you,
Just where we had reached the top
My mind shut against the light –
We were falling, we were sprawled
At the bottom, breathless, sweating.
When you slept I touched your head,
In the dark like Pius praying.

The estate in summer

I stop my ears with abandoned poems.
If something wild from across the centuries
Walked out of the mountains dressed in skins,
Gripping an axe, bewildered, at bay,
Before too long he'd feel himself at home.
Puzzled, they'd soon remember him.
The children and the dogs would gather round

To welcome him with howls, in no time
He'd get a house and a woman to drag by the hair
On Saturday nights, full of firewater.
He'd learn to read *The Mourne Observer*,
Turn in his axe at the police station,
Sign on at the Dole or dig a hole,
Dance on the lawn to Radio One.
I can see him heading off with the boys
This mad July day for the cider and wine,
A head of steam and then pull the stuff,
The town's pride, Cunty Kate and Biddy the Clap.
Maybe I do exaggerate,
But not much. So near and yet so far,
Do they know that I'm against them on their side,
That what I do is half for their sake,
How hard it is for a druid with a headache?
Any day now I could take to the hills.

A baby in the house

She is slim again
And you are on the carpet feeding,
Happy to be dining out.
I watch you follow

My rambling to your father,
Talk of where we've been.
They say how fast you've grown
And now I see you crawl

From strength to strength,
So welcome to the feast
Though soon the walls are gone,
The sky uncertain.

Just watching what you do
And what that does to you
Could tell me all there is to know.
Let me tell your story.

On the bottle too
(It's a celebration)
I'm on my knees to meet you.
Here's looking at you, baby.

Poem

'She lives and works in Dublin. Today's story
Is her first to be published.' Here it's framed
By poetry, four old hands,
Faintly famous, fully fledged.
In the centre there's her photograph
You can tell was taken in a booth
In some arcade or station, slightly blurred
But shining with pure happiness, she's young.
I hope she thought to give her boyfriend one.
I tried to read her story then gave in.
I read the poems. They were quite achieved.

MEDBH
McGUCKIAN

Medbh McGuckian was born in 1950 in
Belfast. Educated at Queen's University, she
presently teaches English at St Patrick's
College in Belfast.

Publications:
Portrait of Joanna, Honest Ulsterman
Publications, 1980
Single Ladies, Interim Press, 1980
Trio Poetry 2 (with Damian Gorman and
Douglas Marshall), Blackstaff Press, 1981
The Flower Master,
Oxford University Press, 1982

The cage-cup

It's been quite a year for strange weather.
From speedy March to slow September,
The drought left firemen sleepless, Ireland
So like Italy Italians came to film it.
Each evening the Egyptian goddess
Swallowed the sun, her innocent
Collective pleasure, never minding his violent temper,
His copious emissions, how he sprinkled
The lawn of space till it became
A deadly freckled junkyard.
Looking at what is most important
Leaves me blind: without leaving my room
I might escape from waves in a Roman cage-cup
Made from a single piece of glass, and sail
My wafer yacht on the solar wind, my watered
Body, my earthy liquid centre, protected
By a crown. Wish me a mission
Trouble free, if I lose contact
To die smiling of exhaustion, the invisible
Child upon a swing so I can almost touch his hands.

The accident

That was the first sign –
The dark flakes appearing in the cups;
(We were not used to such invasions
Of process on our strained and seamless world).

It was a shock, then, to find,
Rinsing out the tea-pot at the tap,
The limp bag eddied like a punctured lung,
Leaves thick as flies in the white corners.

The badger

From Tongue Loanen the lane
Has punched an airfield to the town,
The leaves on the lounge bar of the beach
Like crazy snub-nosed animals.

No map could tell you how to cup
Your hands in this basket
Of rib-caging trees, how to kneel
Over something broken in your youth:

As with all your misty family,
It must be held raw to your eyes,
The immaculate cut of your pin-stripe suit,
Erring faintly on the quiet side.

Faith

My grandmother led us to believe snow
Was an old man in the sky shaking
Feathers down from his mattress over the world.

Her bed in the morning was covered with tiny scales,
Sloughed off in the night from peeling skin;
They floated in a cloud

Of silver husks to the floor, or spun
In the open window like starry litter
Blowing about on the road.

I burned them in a heap, a dream of coins
More than Therese's promised shower of rose petals,
Or Virgil's souls, many as autumn leaves.

Family planning

The sunset dyeing the room so deeply,
I promised myself, tomorrow I would seek
Old-fashioned recipes of herbs and wholemeal,
Work time-honoured patterns, plain and homely style:

Embroidering dimly as dark increased,
I would wear my grandmother's ring and shawl,
And in the evenings watch the firelight fall
Cleanly on my parents' and my children's faces.

The flitting

'You wouldn't believe all this house has cost me –
In body language terms, it has turned me upside down.'
I've been carried from one structure to the other
On a chair of human arms, and liked the feel
Of being weightless, that fraternity of clothes. . .
Now my own life hits me in the throat, the bumps
And cuts of the walls as telling
As the poreholes in strawberries, tomato seeds:
I cover them for safety with these Dutch girls
Making lace, or leaning their almond faces
On their fingers with a mandolin, a dreamy
Chapelled ease abreast this other turquoise-turbanned,
Glancing over her shoulder with parted mouth.

She seems a garden escape in her unconscious
Solidarity with darkness, clove-scented
As an orchid taking fifteen years to bloom,
And turning clockwise as the honeysuckle –
Who knows what importance

She attaches to the hours?
Her narrative secretes its own values, as mine might
If I painted the half of me that welcomes death
In a faggotted dress, in a peacock chair,
No falser biography than our casual talk
Of losing a virginity, or taking a life, and
No less poignant if dying
Should consist in more than waiting.

I postpone my immortality for my children,
Little rock-roses, cushioned
In long-flowering sea-thrift and metrics,
Lacking elemental memories:
I am well-earthed here as the digital clock,
Its numbers flicking into place like overgrown farthings
On a bank where once a train
Ploughed like an emperor living out a myth
Through the cambered flesh of clover and wild carrot.

Chopping

Close your eyes
Unwinding the bitter onion –
Its layers of uncertainty are limited,
Under brown paper its sealed heart sings
To the tune of a hundred lemons.

Today I am feeling up to it:
I bend my throat aside –
There is no pain, only the soft entrances
Again, again, the vegetable's
Finely numbered bones.

Sand

In the ribbed glass of the panelled door
The problem is the rain; but the single clear pane
Shows a fine day, the swept grey paving.
I am so sure there is nothing there,
I touch it to make sure it is not just carelessness,
The mating season gone without a child.

And these then are the leaves, so small
I never noticed how the summer rose them:
Their separate lines are washed and dried like sand.
Today I will shadow someone through the town,
Read bedtime stories, of overexcited schoolgirls,
Their history of never having grown.

Power-cut

The moon is salmon as a postage-stamp
Over the tonsured trees, a rise-and-fall lamp
In a cracked ice ceiling: the cruelty
Of road conditions flushes summer near,
As the storm seal hangs along the pier.

My dishes on the draining-board
Lie at an even keel, the baby lowered
Into his lobster-pot pen; my sponge
Disintegrates in water like a bird's nest,
A permanent wave gone west.

These plotted holes of days my keep-net shades,
Soluble as refuse in canals; the old flame
Of the candle sweats in the night, its hump
A dowager's with bones running thin:
The door butler lets the strangers in.

Up the river

Like a blackbird stealing jewels,
The moon murderer comes
When I am parked up the river, curled with sleeping.

What would happen if the snake
Escaped from the hothouse glass –
The honeycomb ashes of a race?

Nothing can stop us being seen in the water.
There are different kinds of night,
There are different ways of floating.

Chemical Street

The flies are all dead though
I spent the summer killing them,
As curly as the dahlias,
As stuffy as their water.

(I must stress that in this story
I am sixteen years old,
An ageing alsatian,
A classy kind of boat.)

Safe in all the dark,
The poker school, the barbecue.
Love in the park the puckered
Brain of consolation.

I have an hour to kill
Before the set-pieces of the morning.
I recognise the hairstyle
I acquired overnight,

And chained like a key
To my syllabus, my budget,
I hear the sound in Chemical Street
Of what I thought were people.

I am not a morning person,
Not one for wet sleeping-bags,
Or lollipop or ready-concrete men,
Looking everywhere but his face.

The Forties

Officially it's winter,
And blood building has stopped.
My turnover of lovers chafe
With large, tender bruises.

My sturdy crimson lip-salve
Is the net of airmail clouds,
The nylon-stockinged moon
Like a film-star in tears.

And the grapevine rings
Through a matinee of dates,
Where faces rag together
Till their times overlap.

PETER FALLON

Peter Fallon was born in 1951, in Co. Meath
and educated at Trinity College, Dublin. In
1976–77 he was poet-in-residence at
Deerfield Academy, Massachusetts. In 1970
he founded the Gallery Press which publishes
poetry, plays, and short stories
by Irish writers.

Publications:
Co-Incidence of Flesh, Gallery Press, 1972
The First Affair, Gallery Press, 1974
The Speaking Stones, Gallery Press, 1978

As editor:
The First Ten Years (with Dennis
O'Driscoll), Dublin Arts Festival Poetry,
1979
*Soft Day : a miscellany of contemporary
Irish writing* (with Sean Golden), University
of Notre Dame Press, 1979/Wolfhound
Press, 1980
The Writers : A Sense of Ireland (with
Andrew Carpenter) O'Brien Press, 1980

Anniversary

A 30lb pike in the hall
from the day the men
told a serving-girl
that they were after whale

and she believed
and broadcast their success –
stay easy Ahab, Queequeg, Ishmael,
today on Mullagh lake

I must believe
that fish are mythical, or fly,
or climbed the island trees
for there's P. Clarke

and even he's not caught deadbait
though shyly tells
again he won first prize
on competition day

'I'd them tethered a month
and fed on brown bread
and had only to draw them in.'
The day's too bright,

the wave's not right
or something means nothing.
The cormorant is leaving.
It's later a gentlewoman tells

it's August 15th
and we shouldn't be out
for years ago the one man drowned
and another is due to the same waters.

We walk the land
safe until
again we sail frail boats
in the unearthly destinies.

'El Dorado'

The accordionist began
and slowly a band foregathered,
and slowly the dancing started too,
the usual couples courageous,

the women in dresses, the men in suits
weighing the wish and the likelihood.
It was a country dance, the parish priest
was there. The bar ensured a crowd.

Some polka-ed in the foxtrot and 'trotted
in the waltz, and some were jiving expertly.
The girl in the green dress's slips
were showing; she held her handbag as she danced.

Some quickstepped in the slow sets, but those
that found their own kind in the dark danced
close in gestic heaven and learned their loving
in the backs of cars in laneways until dawn.

And some came late and argued for reductions;
others hunted others' passes, straightening up.
One was so drunk he couldn't sit down,
he knelt for the National Anthem

propped by friends, and then drove home.
Next morning in McShane's I asked
if Patsy Boyland had enjoyed the dance
and he replied, 'I don't know. Was I at it?'

Finding the dead

My uncle Peter went to bed
when he heard the dowser
said he charged a fee. And that
was that. In his day men just came,
walked here and there until the rod
sprung to the stream despite themselves,
small talked and went away.

'There's three springs there',
said Brian Keelan and then stood
beyond the new dairy.
A spade dug earth, gravel, mud.
And he asked his fee,
is asking yet I'd say.
My uncle paid for what was earned.

That man found more than water.
He found a friend's gold ring
when it was hidden by St Anthony,
found anything that strayed,
and found the dead.
Not by dredging nor combing
hills, field and forest,

not by firing over the water
nor floating loaves and mercury,
he found the dead,
the lost unentered in God's acre.
Small bits of news,
a piece of clothing – these were clues.
A weight swung like a pendulum

above a map to trace a soul.
Attention full and deep as prayer,
the plumb line swayed as if
a breath fanned and informed him.

He'd point
and there you'd look and find.
That's how they tracked

the bodies in the Blackwater
after all else had failed.
Once he failed himself,
a little girl in Donegal
erred from sight forever
while almost still within it.
That was the mystery

dark as the pool
he sees her in
and which no search can fathom.
In time the unfound dead
will gather in the maps,
will congregate in rituals of recovery
and grow up from their root in him.

Catholics

The man at the bar is cursing women,
he hates his wife and loves his mother,
and tells who'll hear of the whores
he's ridden. When they hadn't a woman
they improvised, himself and another,

behind the ballrooms of their need
they actualised their monstrous art
and in the dark they dreamt of Mary.
And maybe I'm as bad —
I've come for the loan of an ass and cart

and listen to deeds at the Parish Sports
that gorged a greed that knew no bounds,
'Sports is right! That woman's a mother
in England now.' And he escaped. He ran
with the hare and chased with the hounds.

I'm enjoying the stout and the others'
talk but he badgers me,
'We'll have a big night out, both of us,
we'll travel far and find a pair
and none will know, there'll be nobody

the wiser.' And I say 'Aye'
and turn the talk to the ass's age,
her use for foddering, and mention
rain and local news – a death, a sale,
a harvest saved – but he's me in a cage

and starts up again.
'Are you married yourself, a mhic?'
'I was never asked.'
'Sure you've maybe no need, you've maybe
a woman who'll do the trick.'

'You know how it is. . .'
I give nothing away, driftwood
on the tide of his surmise
my answers. But I need the ass
and only say, 'Be good to that good

woman of yours', though I think to myself,
'May your young possess her quality.'
We settle a plan to collect the cart.
He's drunk and I'm linked by one request,
teasing his yes, fending our complicity.

ROBERT
JOHNSTONE

Robert Johnstone was born in Belfast in
1951. He received the Walter Allen Prize for
Poetry in 1973 while a student at The New
University of Ulster. He was co-founder of
Caret, the literary magazine, and has
been associated with the northern review,
Fortnight, since 1974, having become
its co-editor.

Publications:
Our Lives are Swiss,
Ulsterman Publications, 1977
Trio Poetry 1 (with Will Colhoun and David
Park), Blackstaff Press, 1980

Adelaide

The Brits are making a lot
of noise in that damn chopper,
hanging their narrow searchlight
in garish equilibrium
to scan the ghetto for sin.
When they go away again
a proof's still ranged before me,
a carpet of lights from here
to the hills, one each for all
who thought to choose the same life.

I stand with my back against
the writing on the wall, feeling
not safe, but at home at least.
Out there starts Comanche land
with a different class of
graffito, but at night and
distance I'm unable to
discriminate between shade
and nuance. No. Surrendered
to N.I. Rail because
I'm flirting with routine, I've got
nothing to do but wait and
play inside my head with words
for their unnecessary
music.

The postman's bedtime story

Pavements erupt where roots creep
the length of the avenue
underneath our static homes

dismantling the life we built
to accidental beauty,
disinterested of course in

our aesthetic: tonight I
share a function of the trees,
to utter without understanding.

Lost, you've turned your back on me
to fall asleep intact and
thinking of the door between.

Think instead of my hand (which
even now creeps under you)
as a root, disinterested

in your aesthetic, turning
you, if only you'd lie still,
to accidental beauty.

There existed another ending to the Story of O

'Not death, but a new setting, waits for us'
Joseph Brodsky, 'The Candlestick'

I can accept that someone understands
your transparent life in a foreign place,
that he plays your body like an instrument,
that your scent stays on his clothes all day.

He likes to look at you put on your shoes,
he tells you what underwear he wants you to buy,
he watches from the bed as you move
across the room in long sunlight (for we

each agree it's always like autumn there). His
car's parked under the trees. He finds leaves caught
for months behind the bumpers. It's something loose
you fear at the edges of your day, so

on your own you check windows, the glass door
– there's only windows and air between us –
but something indulges a fetish,
occupies gaps when you're gone; for instance,

the miracle of radio, which I
accept, Chopin performed in your empty flat,
polkas that greet your return, for scenes of our
mad love control us, they don't belong.

Can somebody be learning things are
independent? Why else am I returned
to that October in my dream of blood?
Why else would you tremble now, recalling

how I broke glass and wished it was your bones?
But here are your perfumed clothes which wait
innocently still where you left them. See?
Always, really, nothing's been disturbed.

Festival of Mithras

Our foreign troops on the airport bus
take the word tax, ask who we are,
where we've been and where we're going.
We answer box by box.

Where I've been great refineries
ran right through the winter solstice,
burning wealth in the longest nights,
brighter than English cities.

Where I'm going is coming home
where all words wait to be remembered.
I picked some up and left them here
and they became my own.

I tell friends of overgrown gardens
where a hundred flowers might bloom,
predict folk-tales of now, turf-stacks
beside each dwelling,

a street next year where masked children
offer a penny for your thoughts
or cadge good words at every door
to pile high on waste-ground.

Perhaps our litter never gets lost.
For unwrappings, for blowing up things,
we link arms and warm our faces
at the flames of our past.

And out rockets the word Peace,
exploding in stars that make day
until they're consumed utterly
and fall on our heads like nothingness.

Déjà vu

I must be getting old for
I begin to understand
my father's reasons. I turn
with an unexpected love
to his ramshackle business,
the unintended rituals
of his ordinary days.

I must have been ten or less.
Dad was driving the old van
out in the Lagan Valley.
The untouchable birds in big
wicker crates for some arcane
purpose, the men's mysteries:
I thought I'd been there before.

I begin to understand
that some trick of speed, light, on
the road, the fields, the full trees
only seemed from another
similar run we hadn't
made or couldn't remember,
that I'd lost my sense of time.

I begin to recall how
that Protestant country shone
and slept. The workmen could take
time off to wait by their clocks
for us to pause at the spot
and liberate their young birds
that all flapped out in a rush.

I must have looked small beside
my father as he explained
how the pigeons were faithful.
Like magic they circled twice
then headed off correctly
in the direction of home
with a loyalty I didn't know.

PAUL MULDOON

Paul Muldoon was born in Co. Armagh in
1951 and educated at Queen's University,
Belfast. He works as a radio producer with
the BBC in Belfast.

Publications:
New Weather, Faber and Faber, 1973
Mules, Faber and Faber, 1977
Why Brownlee Left, Faber and Faber, 1980

The waking father

My father and I are catching sprickles
Out of the Oona river.
They have us feeling righteous,
The way we have thrown them back.
Our benevolence is astounding.

When my father stood out in the shallows
It occurred to me that
The spricklies might have been piranhas,
The river a red carpet
Rolling out from where he had just stood,

Or I wonder now if he is dead or sleeping.
For if he is dead I would have his grave
Secret and safe,
I would turn the river out of its course,
Lay him in its bed, bring it round again.

    No one would question
That he had treasures or his being a king,
Telling now of the real fish farther down.

The Indians on Alcatraz

Through time their sharp features
Have softened and blurred,
As if they still inhabited
The middle distances,
As if these people have never
Stopped riding hard

In an opposite direction,
The people of the shattered lances
Who have seemed forever going back.
To have willed his reservation,
It is as if they are decided
To be islanders at heart,

As if this island
Has forever been the destination
Of all those dwindling bands.
After the newspaper and TV reports
I want to be glad that
Young Man Afraid Of His Horses Lives

As a brilliant guerrilla fighter,
The weight of his torque
Work like the moon's last quarter,
Though only if he believes,
As I believed of his fathers,
That they would not attack after dark.

Lunch with Pancho Villa

I

'Is it really a revolution, though?'
I reached across the wicker table
With another $10,000 question.
My celebrated pamphleteer,
Co-author of such volumes
As *Blood on the Rose*,
The Dream and the Drums,
And *How It Happened Here*,
Would pour some untroubled Muscatel
And settle back in his cane chair.

'Look, son. Just look around you.
People are getting themselves killed
Left, right and centre
While you do what? Write rondeaux?
There's more to living in this country
Than stars and horses, pigs and trees,
Not that you'd guess it from your poems.
Do you never listen to the news?
You want to get down to something true,
Something a little nearer home.'

I called again later that afternoon,
A quiet suburban street.
'You want to stand back a little
When the world's at your feet.'
I'd have liked to have heard some more
Of his famous revolution.
I rang the bell, and knocked hard
On what I remembered as his front door,
That opened then, as such doors do,
Directly on to a back yard.

II

Not any back yard, I'm bound to say,
And not a thousand miles away
From here. No one's taken in, I'm sure,
By such a mild invention.
But where (I wonder myself) do I stand,
In relation to a table and chair.
The quince-tree I forgot to mention,
That suburban street, the door, the yard –
All made up as I went along
As things that people live among.

And such a person as lived there!
My celebrated pamphleteer!
Of course, I gave it all away
With those preposterous titles.
The Bloody Rose? The Dream and the Drums?
The three-day-wonder of the flowering plum!
Or was I desperately wishing
To have been their other co-author,
Or, at least, to own a first edition
Of *The Boot Boys and Other Battles?*

'When are you going to tell the truth?'
For there's no such book, so far as I know,
As *How it Happened Here,*
Though there may be. There may.
What should I say to this callow youth
Who learned to write last winter –
One of those correspondence courses –
And who's coming to lunch today?
He'll be rambling on, no doubt,
About pigs and trees, stars and horses.

The Centaurs

I can think of William of Orange,
Prince of gasworks-wall and gable-end.
A plodding, snow-white charger
On the green, grassy slopes of the Boyne,
The milk-cart swimming against the current

Of our own backstreet. Hernán Cortez
Is mustering his cavalcade on the pavement,
Lifting his shield like the lid of a garbage-can.
His eyes are fixed on a river of Aztec silver.
He whinnies and paws the earth

For our amazement. And Saul of Tarsus,
The stone he picked up once has grown into a hoof.
He slings the saddle-bags over his haunches,
Lengthening his reins, loosening his girth.
To thunder down the long road to Damascus.

Our Lady of Ardboe

I

Just there, in a corner of the whin-field,
Just where the thistles bloom.
She stood there as in Bethlehem
One night in nineteen fifty-three or four.

The girl leaning over the half-door
Saw the cattle kneel, and herself knelt.

II

I suppose that a farmer's youngest daughter
Might, as well as the next, unravel
The winding road to Christ's navel.

Who's to know what's knowable?
Milk from the Virgin Mother's breast,
A feather off the Holy Ghost?
The fairy thorn? The holy well?

Our simple wish for there being more to life
Than a job, a car, a house, a wife –
The fixity of running water.

For I like to think, as I step these acres,
That a holy well is no more shallow
Nor plummetless than the pools of Shiloh,
The fairy thorn no less true than the Cross.

III

Mother of our Creator, Mother of our Saviour,
Mother most amiable, Mother most admirable.
Virgin most prudent, Virgin most venerable,
Mother inviolate, Mother undefiled.

And I walk waist-deep among purples and golds
With one arm as long as the other.

The wood

for John and Madeline

They tell me how they bought
An hour of silence
From a juke-box in New York
Or San Francisco once,

That now they intend
To go back to their home place
For a bit of peace,

A house overlooking a lake
And a wood for kindling.

'But you can't fell trees
That have stood for as long
As anyone remembers?'

'The wood we have in mind will stand
While it has lost its timber.'

The Narrow Road to The Deep North

A Japanese soldier
Has just stumbled out of the forest.
The war has been over
These thirty years, and he has lost

All but his ceremonial sword.
We offer him an American cigarette.
He takes it without a word.
For all this comes too late. Too late

To break the sword across his knee,
To be right or wrong.
He means to go back to his old farm

And till the land. Though never to deny
The stone its sling,
The blade of grass its one good arm.

The weepies

Most Saturday afternoons
At the local Hippodrome
Saw the Pathe-News rooster,
Then the recurring dream

Of a lonesome drifter
Through uninterrupted range.
Will Hunter, so gifted
He could peel an orange

In a single, fluent gesture,
Was the leader of our gang.
The curtain rose this afternoon
On a lion, not a gong.

When the crippled girl
Who wanted to be a dancer
Met the married man
Who was dying of cancer,

Our hankies unfurled
Like flags of surrender.
I believe something fell asunder
In even Will Hunter's hands.

The Boundary Commission

You remember that village where the border ran
Down the middle of the street,
With the butcher and baker in different states?
Today he remarked how a shower of rain

Had stopped so cleanly across Golightly's lane
It might have been a wall of glass
That had toppled over. He stood there, for ages,
To wonder which side, if any, he should be on.

Ireland

The Volkswagen parked in the gap,
But gently ticking over.
You wonder if it's lovers
And not men hurrying back
Across two fields and a river.

Making the move

When Ulysses braved the wine-dark sea
He left his bow with Penelope,

Who would bend for no one but himself.
I edge along the bookshelf,

Past bad Lord Byron, Raymond Chandler,
Howard Hughes; The Hidden Years,

Past Blaise Pascal, who, bound in hide,
Divined the void to his left side:

Such books as one may think one owns
Unloose themselves like stones

And clatter down into this wider gulf
Between myself and my good wife;

A primus stove, a sleeping-bag,
The bow I bought through a catalogue

When I was thirteen or fourteen
That would bend, and break, for anyone,

Its boyish length of maple upon maple
Unseasoned and unsupple.

Were I embarking on that wine-dark sea
I would bring my bow along with me.

GERARD SMYTH

Gerard Smyth was born in Dublin in 1951.
He works as a journalist for *The Irish Times*.

Publications:
World Without End,
New Writers Press, 1977
Loss and Gain, Raven Arts Press, 1981

Forbidden knowledge

Two screams combine and twist
into an ache of human music.

Ourselves and the watchful owls stop,
absorbed in a trance of fright.

Moonlight measures the obscene trees,
their wooden taste stuns our tender tongues.

Bitterly we break the delicate
twigs and watch the mushrooms rot.

Our shoes are silenced as we move
over the garden's gift of quiet clay.

Where unfinished fruit grows to the age
of ripeness we find forbidden knowledge.

The spirit of a man

i.m. James Clarence Mangan

Black lanes consume the path
that takes him home. Cats' eyes
know fear where drops of sweat
like insects run. The midnight
bell of Christ Church rings.

Long syllables of sound amaze
the frozen stillness in gaps
between the stars. Pity him,
poor poet, with a head full
of words that rhyme. Alone

with time, the ancient silence
of a cave once filled his mouth
with the taste of night's
vast emptiness. The nearest
thing seems far away when

gods destroy the spirit of a man.

Oracles

Illegible dawn, ghost and chimera gone

A rumour at the crossroads
and the feminine scent of flowers
whose virginity is perpetual

Windows with inflammable knowledge
Walls outlasting eternity

The violated sleep of beasts
who dream an entrance to viridian meadows

Light obeys the compass, planting
plausible shadows on the golden dungheap

Builders

Where are the builders who create
our parallel lives?
Their calculations made in haste
The house subsides

Rattling cups and a knife that cuts
without repentance
Much said in consequence
will not be heard

Each sickness cured
by one who cannot heal himself
Immortal wound in mortal flesh

Every distance is a dream
not dreamed of yet
Our ephemeral beatitudes

HARRY CLIFTON

Harry Clifton was born in Dublin in 1952
and educated at University College, Dublin,
where he completed a Master's Degree in
Philosophy in 1975. He taught in Africa for
two years and returned to Ireland in 1978. He
is currently on government secondment to
help with administration of aid programmes
for Indo-Chinese refugees in Thailand.
In 1981 he won the Patrick Kavanagh Award.

Publications:
The Walls of Carthage, Gallery Press, 1977
Office of the Salt Merchant,
Gallery Press, 1979

Metempsychosis

How transfigured I must be,
Being dead, I'm not yet clear.
My soul pines, moping dolefully
About the hospital square.

Soul after pad-footed soul
On the lonely thoroughfares
I've seen abdicate former roles
Already; and I'm hardly here.

I ask – what's left of me,
Queueing for bodily care
At an overworked dispensary
On old, evangelical stairs?

And something that I've become
Sees an aspirant in my stead,
So absent-spirited, glum,
Who keeps hitting his dog on the head

Though leashed. And I cannot help
But wonder what God intends,
That through each querulous yelp
I hear the voice of a friend.

Strange filth

After dark, I came in,
Having scoured
The adamant, fruitless streets
While light was failing.

One lucky hag I saw
Scurry off into the half-light
With her string bag full
Of assorted vegetables.

Before I could reach her,
She was gone. Everywhere
Was a closed shop. I returned
Clean as a whistle,

Except that my feet
Brought in strange filth,
And left it in the hall,
On the stairs, everywhere.

The walls of Carthage

Augustine, ended the priest,
Put it all too well.
Here am I, a priest
In my late forties, still

In the desert, still
Relativity's fool.
Wherever it is the will
Of lycée, college, school,

As here, God to conclude
From premisses, I am sent
For lectures, journées d'études.
Oases of discontent,

Paris, Maynooth, Louvain,
Define my forty-year desert,
My home from home, terrain
Of groundless visions, assert

The same topography
As he, Augustine, mapped.
Godless in Carthage city,
A dialectician, trapped

In a waste of comparisons,
His speech is my speech, speech
Of failure, of a man
Old enough now to preach

Of a God he may never know
Under the sun – a mirage.
So, with Augustine I tell you,
Alexandria, Carthage,

We, in inferior reason,
Travel until we fall,
To compare, in a desert season,
The beauty of their walls.

The casuist

True, there were black souls in the families
Of the Thirties. Dig up sacred ground.
The facts are there. I root my recent homilies
In suchlike exhumations, where I found

One day – You've heard this? – burying one dead
Another dead below. And stooping down,
I picked an ancient glitter from his head.
We closed the grave. At dinner in the town.

Where genealogy forked I found his name,
Old living quarters. When the skeleton-widow
Gave me entrance, I produced her shame –
A golden tack. As if her husband's shadow

Leaned in the doorway. 'God has found me out!'
She muttered. All his alcoholic years,
Her hatred bottled, stoppered with this doubt –
Inheres there value in what just appears?

Maybe I am, as you've always said I am,
A guilty man, interpreting a crooked tree
In an old way. I know, you'd have me damned
For reaching into graves unflinchingly

Nor letting overtones corrupt the savour
Of my literal dinners – hear me out –
Prose intellect. The facts are in whose favour?
In the end, that woman murdered doubt

By murdering faith. It's not ridiculous.
One night, she got her tack inside his skull.
What happened proved her unperspicuous.
The end was not the end, but just a lull

Between her spurning the validity
I speak for, and the day God chose to amend
Her dulness, pierced with a golden quiddity.
The facts *are* loaded. Where does this tree end?

English lesson

The blind yellow walls
Of a skylit classroom, which the janitors
Cleaned overnight, and the smell
Of disinfected floor.

And the arranged faces
In a morning class begun
At time understood, confront and disgrace
The latecomers, as one by one,

From stained lavatories
Of urine and cigarette smoke
They enter, rehearsed in dirty jokes
And the poetry of the day,

Resigning, without a word,
Prerogative to my talk,
My english, what I write on a razed blackboard,
My characters of chalk.

Loneliness in the Tropics

No one coming home
From North, South, East or West
To the unlit aerodrome
Tonight. . . So they can rest,

The black nightwatchmen,
Behind deserted transit shacks
And talk. They wave again
As I reach the end of the airfield. . . I walk back,

My mind full of empty spaces,
Billowing like a windsock
On a pole. Already this restlessness,
An hour old by the clock,

Is wearing off. . . I can sleep it off
After German beer
At the village whorehouse, if they have enough –
I have been here a year.

Catarrh

Imagine that smell
On the high escarpment, forty miles from town,
Where eighty donkeys fell
In the Rainy Season. . . how can I walk and disown,

Around here, what the vultures do?
Called Health Inspectors,
Legalised, like beautiful African avenues,
African slums, death and protection

Incarnate in the same
Untouchables. . . Under their wing
I see how the leprous and maimed
Turned professional beggar, how minor tragedies cling,

Repeat themselves
From tribesman to tribesman – civilised diseases,
Prophylactic shelves
Of Medicine Men, Mahomet in scuffles with Jesus

Tonight on the autumn streets
As Rhamadhan ends. . .
Upstaging their African roots
At the Hotel Terminus, the Sahara All Stars Band

Is tuning up. I pity the prostitute,
Deprived of name and culture,
Whose life is a first-floor room there, a free cigarette
When the buses arrive, I envy the code of the vulture

Who followed the tribes into town
Like a memory, a past into which elders rot
As the Rains die down
And the New Moon shines. They've laid the dead within earshot

Of evening prayers, in ultraviolet rays
From amplified mosques. Ironic sophistication –
Catarrhine faces
Streaming with catarrh. . . No further dispensation,

Now, for the sons to fulfill,
To carry their own dead fathers
On their backs, back into the obsolete hills
Where vultures still gather.

Magyar coat

Before I could walk, I was wheeled –
Felt vaguely eternal, Mother behind me a mystery
Out of the shadow of whose magyar coat I crawled,
Started making history.

Grannie confused me, embittered
By ceaseless politics. Mother changed religion
In the Cold War, and my vague eternity shattered –
It must have been about then.

Behind long hair, dark glasses,
I hid myself, a student walking the streets
Of East Berlin, a child of the privileged classes,
Trying to make opposites meet.

The prostitutes in the lights
Of the motor showrooms, along Potsdamerstrasse
Kept their hours, from afternoon into night,
As back to the West I passed

Amid human confusion –
Coated like magyars, women of yesteryear
Swarmed in the Eastern Sector, Mother's old fashions –
The world must be going nowhere. . .

'. . .Your magyar coat, your magyar coat,
What did I want to say?. . . Oh nothing, some nonsense. . .'
Grannie is pestering Mother. It sticks in my throat,
Like trying to explain my presence

By an image, at history's
Real checkpoints, checkpoints I can't circumvent –
Where nonsense was good enough for eternal mystery,
I want to be sure what is meant.

GERALD DAWE

Gerald Dawe was born in Belfast in 1952 and
educated at Orangefield Boys' School, the
New University of Ulster, and University
College, Galway, where he graduated with a
Master of Arts degree in 1978.
In 1980 he received an Arts Council
Bursary. He now lives in Galway.

Publications:
Sheltering Places, Blackstaff Press, 1978

Count

My only problem is your death
when the radio was stuttering
over breakfast in this flat

the predicted west gale welting
round our postage-stamp garden,
a fat crow crouched under the wall,

and the early morning warmth
dazed, an impractical consciousness
footering with cups, toast laid

in their apparent order
when first I heard your name.
It sounded crazy, somehow or other

as incoherent as a dream:
your name, age, place of birth,
and then the on-the-spot commentary

reasoning details of why and how they
waited in a car for you coming out
of a huckster-shop with cigarettes

And pumped six bullets: five when you
sprawled on the street. It's hard to
make that count. The boy that did it

was a few years younger. Twenty years,
six bullets, nine in the morning.
I toy like a child with these numbers.

Sheltering Places

It's been pelting down
all night the kind
of rain that drenches
to the bone

and a dirtstorm
in the car park.
The hot wind carries
thunder making girls

scream and old men
count the seconds,
improvising distance
as you shout to

turn the lights out,
pull down the blinds
so that lightning can't
get in and frazzle us up

in the curtain-dark room
the rumbles near and
shattering flashes
make everything go numb.

The storm is reaching
home territory, stretching
over the hills down
into our sheltering places.

Premonition

for Seamus Deane

At the raw tree root,
nestling, the entranced neck

seizes premoniton.
A great wing flap, the swan

tramples water
and across the still morning

is stretched in a feud
of exultation.

Memory

It is a desert of rock
the rain has finally withered
till we are left black
dots on a shrinking island.

We come like pilgrims
wandering at night through
the dim landscape. A blue
horizon lurks behind whin-

bushes and narrows to pass
the pitch-black valley.
We are at home: a place as
man-forsaken as this must

carry like the trees a silent
immaculate history. Stones
shift under the cliff's
shadow. We listen to crows

soldiering through night.
Nearby the tide closes in –
master of the forgotten thing.

The sleepwalker

'. . . this is not the place to deplore
the miseries of our century but to
congratulate you on the ingenious
arguments you found in proof of Truth.'
Kepler to Galileo

'I am the last man on earth
        you could call on,
all my time spent Moon-
        Gazing from an attic window,

particular about the star
        formations. Like my imagination
the World is done for.
        See when I turn from the great

Firmament my fate is
        telescoped: dirty streets
full of louts about to blast
        each other into diabolic

Eternity. But I, sublime
    worshipper of alternative gods,
have seen behind the future
    and found it to be wanting,

(my proof is my fear). Thus
    I stare at time
out of hand. In No-Man's-Land.'

Morning start

for Thomas Kilroy

Like the nails of a hand
    ticking my window,
a moth persists. I know
    the great horse stands

by the broken door
    restless as the light,
no more than a candle,
    flickers in the night.

One carries news from
    home, the other seems
to wait beneath my room.
    I ride madcapped dreams

as men and night close
    in, limbless and dumb,
their memories earthed
    to blasted corner stone,

but wake to the bright
     isolation of birds,
and the morning start –
     a smattering of words.

At the Mill, Ballyshrule, Co. Galway

The constitutional

A stroll along the prom –
Bangor is a mass of lights,
rafts bob on the fabulous
tide away out and old faces
glint behind bay windows.

The parlours get dark
and curtains stay back
on rowing boats chained
for the night. Evening
dies on prayerbooks and
heirloom bibles stacked

on hallstands. You read
The People's Friend, the
children are fast asleep.
Further down the cooling
sand jellyfish like beached
mines and fridges in ice-

cream shops hum innocently.
The grand parades are full
of castaways fumbling love-
acts and the bronze gongs
wait upon their Atlases
to be finally struck.

WILLIAM PESKETT

William Peskett was born in Cambridge in
1952 but came to Belfast in 1959. He was
educated at The Royal Belfast Academical
Institution and Christ's College, Cambridge.
He taught biology for five years in a school
in Suffolk and now works as a journalist in
London. He won an Eric Gregory Award
in 1976.

Publications:
The Nightowl's Dissection,
Secker and Warburg, 1975
Survivors, Secker and Warburg, 1980

The nightowl

The nightowl preys
the breadth of the moon,
confronts the crossfire
between the men above
and the men below.

The nightowl escapes
to the dark side.
I will not pursue him
or bring him down to earth.
For me his secrets soar.

The question of time

Where on earth
has the stumbling mammoth gone?
that giant tripper over nations
who used to think
the world was his
after the succulent brontosaurus.

The ages shed no tears for me.
I am not their resting
but their passing through,
left to watch
the intricate bees
in their noble art of dance.

From Belfast to Suffolk

First the pleasures fire the heart –
sutures of oak and elm
divide acres of polyploid grasses
into skull plates
to civilise every corner of the country.
Driving from the Low House
we might pass a dozen churches,
towers that indicate
walking distance across the fields
set alight with beacons.

More honest than the view from innocence
where plumes of smoke along the skyline
describe another operation,
here, the factory workers of the earth
are burning stubble,
purifying the season.
Later, driving tractors in the dark
the sharp spot-light turns
a glistening edge of soil
in long tracks across the land.

The night-police don't scare me here.
Like the man who, in the end,
neglects his mother for his wife
a faithfulness supersedes
the pleasures of the moon.
This demilitarised home
protects me like the other –
its signpost names pronounceable,
its fields the map
in my head.

Moths

Moths are hopeless in the air,
they are wild uncomfortable
companions to the wind,
enjoying the randomness of flight.

Moths have no face.
Smiling, I always think they
must drink light.
A cloud of them can absorb the moon.

The female moth is like the male.
When you crush it,
it doesn't bleed –
it sprinkles your hands with talcum.

The inheritors

for Paul Muldoon

And the ones that got tough
ripped the soft parts
from the sea.
With a spine and a jaw
they pressed a clear advantage,
picking bones with ones
whose shadows met their own.
Gasping, they broke the surface.

The ones that had legs
came up where there was nothing.
Starting as one,
they split into bands

and savaged the green ground.
Ambivalent, they slid in the swamp
from home to home, cleverer,
keeping their options open.

The ones that could crawl
stood up and dried
the afterbirth from their backs.
Somehow they grew to break
the treaty of the land:
becoming gross they tore
the flesh of the sinless
and took three elements in their stride.

The ones that were feathered
came to know the slaughter
of the plain. Gliding from cliffs
they tumbled to the line of flight.
Innocent in the air, their shapes
against the sun began to drop –
below, their claws ripped fur
from nervous carcasses.

And the ones that gave suck
ran like warm blood
through high branches.
With a crib for their young
their lives might have been maternal
but for precedent. Not born
to run with the innocent,
inheritors, we kill.

Cri de coeur

Imagine cutting your wrists
and, like puffs of smoke
from a paratrooper's heels,
bleeding in the bath
from your peripheral circulation.

It's the act of a man
not getting to the heart
of the matter:
cries echo within the tiled walls,
smoke signals in still water.

At Pamukkale

All's quiet in Necropolis –
a host of easy consciences
lies confidently contained
in stone sarcophagi.

Each tomb has trapped
its measure of unbroken dark,
each memory dated
like a musty bloom of wine.

By cracking marble you could smash
the casks from these legacies
and release the moment
like clear blocks from a tray of ice,

but taking illicit gasps
of ancient air to no effect.
The experience is gone,
its record in the face of stone.

Now we fill the volumes of the day
with our loud lives.
Hastily we take a bit of time
and leave no trace.

Below Necropolis, beneath the gaze,
on the cotton cliffs
a stream gives up its load of lime
to monumental clouds of stone.

MATTHEW
SWEENEY

Matthew Sweeney was born in Donegal in
1952 and has lived in London or Southern
Germany since 1973.

Publications:
A Dream of Maps, Raven Arts Press, 1981

Astronomy

It's not my birthday, & amnesties
are not acquired by prophets,
so I sit here on the sea-front
in Aberystwyth, out of season.

This is my posting. Crowds
of shadows stand before me,
the perfect audience. And gulls,
waves. I can preach here.

Can stand on the band-pavilion
each middday, drone my news.
Hecklers are banished. I prefer that;
and applause always worried me.

Yet sometimes in the sea-air I ponder
my despatch here. By cynics.
On a train; to stay here
till I invent laughter.

As if I fake the future!
No matter. I continue; my curved
telescope still functions . . .
dark footsteps, growing.

Astronomy; that sharp star
is Venus, its clouds of gas.
I have seen through all
I am excess.

Armada

A big wind, like a bible story.
The sea thrown at Donegal.
Boys keeping sheep from cliffs
saw ships appear, like darker
boys saw three caravels.

A big wind; hulls broken.
Men blown ashore.
And again that spun Latin –
exchanged with priests. This time
no Cortez rode inland.

A thousand men trickled
to the fort of the Gaelic chief.
Were fed there; wintered
among redhaired curious women.
And picked at their ruined ships.

Till one jigsaw ship
swung out for Scotland.
Waters swarmed off Antrim,
filled its sails.
Gulls flew back to Spain.

The television creature speaks

I am behind the screen
of your television
in a nest of glass & steel.
I reside here.
Don't be dismayed
if I speak suddenly
after all these years,
if you hear me
beyond the dialogue
in another ear. Don't
come with points of light
probing to see me.
You will not. Yet I'm here
even when the screen
shrinks to a dot
& beyond. I'm here
with nothing to do
but watch you. How
you lounge in the grey glow
for hours, while work nags
unheeded. How you add
your chuckle to the comic's
taped applause. Or speed
your heart to deaths
dressed-up in wax, drenched
with a bad painter's red.
And you cross your legs,
gargle whisky, as the cold
stays outside.
I watch you now
through shots where death
climbs from within:
a girl a child's size –
a child in her arms
so thin the camera
shows his x-ray.

Two roots & a frog
are what they'll eat
and they are smiling.
Two roots & a frog
found in a field with
an unburied skull & bones.
I see your mind wander –
you don't like this . . .
Saturn, or some eastern place.
You are hungry. Your feet
shake the floor, & you switch off
while a young doctor
shakes his head at hope.
But wait, I am still here.
Watch the dead screen
beyond your mirrored face,
look: a large bird is running
across the sand.
Don't you recognise him?
He is not equipped to fly.

The window

There would be chairs there, at the window
like wagons, all in a ring.
For it's survival tactics. A lit fire,
certainly, & a pot of tea prepared.
And the net curtains kept black & dusty –
camouflage. No one must be seen.

Their number is unknown, small perhaps
as threatened species are. They speak little;
a background music plays on Radio 3.
Cars chug past at all hours.

Pens & notebooks would be somewhere,
and nearby, a camera & telephone.

For years they have done this –
no strangers to blue strafe lights.
Though the law is a sieve, merely,
with the holes worn large.
Portraits line the walls, a lineal row.
Night falls. Their duty is begun.

Funny face

Into the length of a Sunday,
as if work had stopped to greet,
you came. Blue & moored
till that first breath, then free
in the vast space of light.
You squealed like a hater, as indeed
you were, then nothing for it,
whimpered into silence.

Now there is time to watch you:
child from nowhere, statue
chipped from love & touched alive.
Funny face. A conch in your pram.
Neat as a grasshopper, yet still
those kicking legs go nowhere.
Fingernails of onyx,
your palm scarred with life.

Neophyte, let it pass slowly.
Let your spotlight eyes deter
the hooded boys, their knives that stop.
Let no one waste your name
nor surgeons grope inside you.
Let your voice erase the nightmare:
falling masonry, air that kills,
the starred map-fed men.

THOMAS
McCARTHY

Thomas McCarthy was born in
Co. Waterford in 1954 and was educated at
University College, Cork. He now works with
the Cork City Library. He won the Patrick
Kavanagh Award in 1977 and the following
year received an Arts Council Bursary. In
1978 he was a Fellow of the Iowa University
Writing Programme.

Publications:
The First Convention, Dolmen, 1978
The Sorrow-Garden, Anvil Press, 1981

State funeral

*'Parnell will never come again, he said. He's there, all that
was mortal of him. Peace to his ashes.'*
James Joyce, *Ulysses*

That August afternoon the family
Gathered. There was a native *déjà-vu*
Of Funeral when we settled against the couch
On our sunburnt knees. We gripped mugs of tea
Tightly and soaked the TV spectacle;
The boxed ritual in our living-room.

My father recited prayers of memory.
Of monster meetings, blazing tar-barrels
Planted outside Free-State homes, the Broy-
Harriers pushing through a crowd, Blueshirts;
And, after the war, De Valera's words
Making Churchill's imperial palette blur.

What I remember is one decade of darkness,
A mind-stifling boredom; long summers
For blackberry picking and churning cream,
Winters for saving timber or setting lines
And snares: none of the joys of here and now
With its instant jam, instant heat and cream:

It was a landscape for old men. Today
They lowered the tallest one, tidied him
Away while his people watched quietly.
In the end he had retreated to the first dream,
Caning truth. I think of his austere grandeur;
Taut sadness, like old heroes he had imagined.

Brown copy

for Bríd

Above my fireplace, a brown
engraving, Bríd's pencil copy
held fast with a pin:

in the firelight I can
see grey figures moving
on a bleaching-green

gathering bright linen;
carefully playing it in
like valuable fishing-line:

in the left corner
is a clump of trees
arranged like a Japanese

display, rigid verticals
pointing to heaven, weaker
branches spreading widely.

Between those lines
a worker stumbles
under a burden of cloth.

The builder of statues

from Pablo Neruda

I am the builder of statues,
with no fixed face, no name –
to see my many faces you must
leap into the brambles, climb
the high wall; suffer the work.

And they mean nothing; never meant
anything, but to be born there;
mere sand, surviving silent time.
These statues – on which I wore
out so many fingernails, hands

and arms – cannot say a single
word, a single syllable from
that great aromatic crater.
They are what I was, gazing out
at the waves; stone of my image.

But smaller malign gods, the fish,
the birds that disturbed my days,
are something different. They break
the stature of once-living images:
they feed on our singing harvest –

the harvest of flesh that is
consumed; flowers, dead without
seed, in the belly of an island:
where the statues, worked-clay, are
playing sentry with huge, dead eyes.

Breaking Garden

He's reluctant to move; old campaigner
Familiar with siege. He had spent hours
On violent streets during the Thirties,
Refusing to move despite batons and gas:
But this is the year of forced migration;
Letters, books are stuffed in bags like grain,
Pictures and paperweights, crumbling squadrons
Of files await the retreating campaign.

She's more resigned. Quiet in acquiesence:
She moves quickly between rows of growth,
Deciding which plants must stay. I watched her
For days. With two sheepdogs for lieutenants
She tested the tallest stems; made a note
Of the tough ones, those likely to endure.

My father, reading

The wide lamps at his bedside table would burn
while he fought nervously between books and dream.
The house fell asleep before his hands reached out.

In daylight our town pursued its gossip-lines
while our father drank his tea and studied on:
his sons would come home to an absence of words
while their lives cried out to be taken in hand.

My father became famous on his word-journeys,
sailing (on extended leave), with Scott, avenging
all crime with *Four Just Men*. Every book I open
brings him to the window, to strain his weak eyes
and answer our long calls with a wave of his pen.

Last days in the Party

You let the razor-wound bleed in the warm
Wet silence. In the stains on your bright
Shirt I could gauge developing sorrows:
Earlier, you had forgotten the discussion
Papers, abandoned them in the locked car
As if they were blood-hardened criminals.

You planned to leave with dignity: after
Years of election committees and country
Meetings you had hoped for an after-glow
Of respect, a friendly exchange of roles:
Instead, you discovered a packed meeting,
Delegates like matadors waiting for blood.

Ten years ago you brought me to the first
Conference. Then you handled words calmly,
Juggled with complaints from the platform,
Tied hostilities neatly on a long string
Of language. Trapped in that jungle of old
Men, I made a beacon of your word-play.

Tonight, Father, master of tough language,
It's you I find trapped on a tightening
Syntax; pulled out of depth. The young man
In the trendy suit laughs when he takes
Your place. His broad smile is your dead
Old cheer; a flourish without permanence.

Listening to novelists

I. Francis Stuart

He has been talking about moments of awakening,
odd summer days when one's eye follows light
into an expanded purpose, while he leans
on an elbow that creaks under ages of grief.
A beautiful woman asks the first question;
the words leave her lips like an exuded
maple-syrup. They curve about the whole room,
licking the audience with a wifely moisture.

A professor taking a pencil from his pocket
offers a sterner question. He wants
to know about the scourge of History. 'Tell us,'
he demands, 'about your concept of commitment.'
The novelist stares through the window for a way
out of history; beech in leaf, girls in spring clothes.

II. Isaac Bashevis Singer

Lying in bed in the freezing foreign city;
straining through the buzz of an air-conditioner,
I can hear his voice on wings of static –
the voice like a daemon that survived all War.
He felt that he had been part of an unlikely
adventure that happened just the same. All
he had wanted was to write for his own hurt
language, but his love-cup spilled over us all.

'Mr Singer, what's good writing?' the young girl
asks, her voice so American and untroubled:
'I'll tell you what,' he answers. 'It's a book
that prevents you from getting sleep.' She says
that's *too* simple. 'Well,' he says, 'since I'm not
obliged to be obscure or profound, I tell the truth.'

AIDAN CARL
MATHEWS

Aidan Carl Mathews was born in Dublin in
1956 and educated at Trinity College,
Dublin, where he is reading for a Master's
Degree. He received the Patrick Kavanagh
Award in 1976 and in 1978 won the
Macaulay Fellowship.

Publications:
Windfalls, Dolmen, 1979

Cave-painter

A rope of rushlight wavers
On a damp ledge of sandstone.
His knuckle shapes an antler,
Tusks like a quarter moon.
Tomorrow's prey is promised
In the quarry of his art.

I was a boy-scout when
Stale air in his studio
Rushed on a probing torch.
A doctor in a caravan
Named with a number
A pestle stained with pigment.

Now, in a locked bedroom,
On the edge of utterance,
I ask strength of the dead;
Fearing a cave-in, nearing
A warm odour of wolfskin,
Glistening bone, faeces.

The train

After an hour, our eyes
Intent upon avoiding,
We exhaust strangeness, smile.
Her scarf attempts to hide
A birthmark like a lovebite
Where the throat tilts upward.

I name her in italics
Inked on a paper tag.
Mured in her warm legend,
She rests on her reflection.
A hard, bronchitic gust
Stalls on the stained window.

Were the long carriage empty
Of three nuns, a student
Chic in a gypsy skirt,
I would reach out until
My fingers touched pale lobes,
The stray crease of her hair.

Night

I switch off the light, afraid
Of what comes after night prayer.
Even on knees by the bedside,
Half-way through a Hail Mary,
No crucifix can halt
The thought or the suggestion.

I think of bulking rock,
The blunt knock of mallets.
A soldier threw the dice,
Another picked his nails.
A shape slung on a cross;
Wrists, ribcage slackened.

In the distinct darkness,
Other pictures gather.
Suburbs in the distance
Slope to a camp brothel.
Raucous laughter, loiterers;
Merge of damp bodies.

What of the pitted forehead,
Lips that had spoken love,
Feet lashed to a splinter?
No need to reckon why
The night brings perspiration,
Two beckoning impulses.

The volcano

Heat in the high nineties, the light hurting;
I stand, petrified, on the black lip, gouged
Rigour of stone hurt beyond protest.
Cordite harms my nostrils, my eyes moisten.
It happened here, I am told, consider
The poise of his last gesture: how he stripped,

Combed his moustache with a toothbrush, tied
The boilersuit with parcel string, and pitched,
Like a shot bird, into the crater. And did
The fall redeem the failure that decreed?
Aeschylus died two thousand years ago.
We have unlearned the necessary gesture.

The shadows prosper, requisition this
Remnant of genesis and now I know
The god we worship was never gentle.
Staring at bottles on the waterfront,
Municipal labourers say he used
Those words, or words like them, and play poker.

The square

We reach the sixth stop on our five-day tour,
Of considerable historical importance.
The guide informs us in four languages
We can explore but please be back by three.
We group around a pump for photographs.
The square itself is an unswept mess,
Taken in at a glance. That Nazis sacked

And Xenophon makes mention of a cult
Is entered on a postcard. We forget
Exhausted dogs nosing the lids of bins,
A ravel of election manifestoes.
You sip a coke, I smoke a cigarette,
Empty a bag of breadcrumbs for the birds.
A thin child in a faded cotton dress,

Her eyes enormous, watches from a doorway.
Perhaps she has not seen long hair before.
I smile at her. She stiffens, turns aside,
Appears again as the bus revs up.
I watch her from the air-conditioned coach,
Gathering butts, leftovers into a bag.
A waiter shouts from the cash register.

I think we may have passed Olympia,
The terraced beehives littering Naupactos,
The olive groves of Amfissa. At least,
That was our paid prospectus but I can't
Remember many other stops we made. For days
And what was worse for nights, a pair of eyes,
A pair of darting hands gathering crusts.

159

An answer

The hermits have left Meru, Mr Yeats:
No forwarding address. They are gone
Into reality of desolation.

We did not choose this patrimony, sir,
And are dismayed by the inheritance.
The more so since you died intestate.

Legionary

Earning his keep, a perpetual limp,
Some unknown acre annexed for the empire,
Moor the perspiring mistral thrashed.
Rain on his nape was sharp as javelins.

Odour of burnt timber in his nostrils,
Charred gander in the camp fire. At home,
She opened her legs and he remembered
His mate on the ramparts, kneecaps fractured.

Remedies emptied his wool pockets.
Fitful, he stared at a soiled jerkin,
Tasting infection in his own flesh.
At such times his wife would not come near him.

June the Seventh

In Portugal today the Government
Ordered the troops to man the barricades.
Photos in the evening papers show me
An opened jugular, a thin spittle of blood.
I turn the page to read about a scandal.

This afternoon I wheeled a covered corpse
Into the morgue. A mother sat in tears
While nurses dressed a gash in her son's knee.
'Your father told you not to go in there.'
Later the boy goes home to a beating.

And in the evening when I came to you,
I found you fast asleep. Your light brown hair
Trailed from the quilt over the cast iron.
I found a note on the kitchen table:
The milk has gone off. Please buy a bottle.

Minding Ruth

for Seamus Deane

She wreaks such havoc in my library,
It will take ages to set it right –
A Visigoth in a pinafore

Who, weakening, plonks herself
On the works of Friedrich Nietzsche,
And pines for her mother.

She's been at it all morning,
Duck-arsed in my History section
Like a refugee among rubble,

161

Or, fled to the toilet, calling
In a panic that the seat is cold.
But now she relents under biscuits

To extemporise grace notes,
And sketch with a blue crayon
Arrow after arrow leading nowhere.

My small surprise of language,
I cherish you like an injury
And would swear by you at this moment

For your brisk chatter brings me
Chapter and verse, you restore
The city itself, novel and humming,

Which I enter as a civilian
Who plants his landscape with place names.
It stands an instant, and fades.

Her hands sip at my cuff. She cranes,
Perturbedly, with a book held open
At plates from Warsaw in the last war.

Why is the man with the long beard
Eating his booboos? And I stare
At the old rabbi squatting in turds

Among happy soldiers who die laughing,
The young one clapping: you can see
A wedding band flash on his finger.

BIBLIOGRAPHICAL NOTE

Andrew Carpenter and Peter Fallon (eds) *The Writers*, O'Brien
   Press, 1980
Douglas Dunn (ed.) *Two Decades of Irish Writing*, Carcanet, 1975
Sean Lucy (ed.) *Irish Poets in English*, Mercier, 1972
John Montague (ed.) *The Faber Book of Irish Verse*, Faber 1974 &
   1978

Irish Poetry Publishers
Blackstaff Press, 144 University Street, Belfast 7
Dolmen Press, The Lodge, Mountrath, Portlaoise, Ireland
Gallery Press, 19 Oakdown Road, Dublin 14
Goldsmith Press, The Curragh, Kildare
New Writers Press, 61 Clarence Mangan Road, Dublin 8
Raven Arts Press, 31 North Frederick Street, Dublin I

Other poetry outlets in Ireland
Cork Review, 8 Bridge Street, Cork
Cyphers, 3 Selskar Terrace, Ranelagh, Dublin 6
Era (occasional), The Curragh, Kildare
Honest Ulsterman, 70 Eglantine Avenue, Belfast 9
Innti, 1 Faiche na Coirre Baine, Seanchill, Baile Atha Cliath
Lace Curtain (occasional), 61 Clarence Mangan Road, Dublin 8
'New Irish Writing', *The Irish Press*, Burgh Quay, Dublin
Poetry Ireland Review, The Nook, Mornington, Co. Meath
Stony Thursday Book (annual), 59 William Street, Limerick
Threshold, Lyric Theatre, Ridgeway Street, Belfast 7

Some magazines with special 'Irish Poetry' issues/supplements
Aquarius, 12, 1980
Bananas, no. 26, April 1981
Helix, nos. 5 & 6, Feb–Aug 1980
Lines Review, nos. 52 & 53, May 1975
The Literary Review, vol. 22 no. 2, Winter 1979
Ploughshares, vol. 6 no 1., 1980
Sewanee Review, vol. LXXXIV no. 1, Winter 1976
Stand, vol. 19 no. 2, 1978

Essays and articles related to contemporary Irish poetry regularly
appear in magazines such as *Crane Bag*, *Eire/Ireland* and *Irish
University Review*.

ACKNOWLEDGEMENTS

Acknowledgements are due to the following for permission to reprint poems in this anthology:

For poems by Eavan Boland: to Allen Figgis ('Belfast Vs Dublin' from *New Territory*); and to Arlen House ('The war horse', 'Child of our time' and 'Conversation with an Inspector of Taxes' from *The War Horse*; 'Solitary' from *In Her Own Image*; 'A ballad of beauty and time' from *Night Feed*).

For poems by Ciarán Carson: to The Blackstaff Press Ltd ('The Half-Moon Lake', 'O'Carolan's complaint', 'Linen', 'The bomb disposal' and 'Our country cousins' from *The New Estate*); and to Ulsterman Publications Ltd ('Visitors', 'Smithfield' and 'East of Cairo' from *The Lost Explorer*).

For poems by Harry Clifton: to The Gallery Press ('Strange filth', 'Metempsychosis', 'The walls of Carthage' and 'The casuist' from *The Walls of Carthage*; 'English lesson', 'Catarrh', 'Loneliness in the Tropics' and 'Magyar coat' from *Office of the Salt Merchant*).

For poems by Gerald Dawe: to The Blackstaff Press Ltd ('Sheltering places', 'Count', 'Premonition' and 'Memory' from *Sheltering Places*); and to the author ('The sleepwalker', 'Morning start' and 'The Constitutional').

For poems by Paul Durcan: to Dublin Magazine Press ('November 1976' and 'The girl with the keys to Pearse's Cottage' from *O Westport in the Light of Asia Minor*); to The Gallery Press ('The weeping headstones of the Isaac Becketts' and 'What is a Protestant, Daddy?' from *Teresa's Bar*); to Profile Press ('Going home to Mayo, Winter, 1949', 'Backside to the wind', 'Poetry, a natural thing', 'Making love outside Áras an Uachtaráin' and 'In memory: The Miami Showband: massacred 31 July 1975' from *Sam's Cross*); and to Raven Arts Press ('Death in the quadrangle', 'For My Lord Tennyson I Shall Lay Down My Life' and 'The death by heroin of Sid Vicious' from *Jesus, Break His Fall*).

For poems by Peter Fallon: to The Gallery Press ('"El Dorado"', 'Anniversary' and 'Finding the dead' from *The Speaking Stones*); and to the author ('Catholics').

For poems by Michael Foley: to The Blackstaff Press Ltd ('True life love stories', 'Through the gateless gate' and 'I remember Adlestrop' from *True Life Love Stories*; 'Corbière's eternal feminine' from *The GO Situation*); and to the author ('Poor people in church').

For poems by Robert Johnstone: to Ulsterman Publications Ltd ('The postman's bedtime story' from *Our Lives Are Swiss*); to The Blackstaff Press Ltd ('Adelaide' and 'There existed another ending to the Story of O' from *Trio Poetry 1*); and to the author ('Festival of Mithras' and 'Déjà vu').

For poems by Thomas McCarthy: to The Dolmen Press Ltd ('State funeral', 'Brown copy', 'The builder of statues', 'Breaking Garden' and 'Last days in the Party' from *The First Convention*); and to Anvil Books Ltd ('My father, reading' and 'Listening to novelists' from *The Sorrow-Garden*).

For poems by Medbh McGuckian: to Oxford University Press ('The flitting' and 'Power-cut' from *The Flower-Master*); and to Ulsterman Publications Ltd ('The cage-cup', 'The accident', 'Faith', 'Family planning', 'The badger', 'Chopping', 'Sand', 'Up the river', 'Chemical Street' and 'The Forties' from *Portrait of Joanna*).

For poems by Aidan Carl Mathews: to The Dolmen Press Ltd ('Cave painter', 'The train', 'Night', 'The volcano', 'The square', 'An answer', 'Legionary' and 'June the Seventh' from *Windfalls*); and to the author ('Minding Ruth').

For poems by Hugh Maxton: to The Dolmen Press Ltd (*The Noise of the Fields*).

For poems by Paul Muldoon: to Faber and Faber Ltd ('The waking father' and 'The Indians on Alcatraz' from *New Weather*; 'Lunch

168

with Pancho Villa', 'Our Lady of Ardboe', 'The Centaurs', 'The wood', and 'The Narrow Road to The Deep North' from *Mules*; 'The weepies', 'The Boundary Commission', 'Ireland' and 'Making the move' from *Why Brownlee Left*).

For poems by Paul Murray: to New Writers' Press (*Ritual Poems*, reprinted by The Dolmen Press Ltd in *Rites and Meditations*).

For poems by Frank Ormsby: to Oxford University Press ('Landscape with figures', 'Sheepman', 'After Mass', 'The edge of war', 'Islands', 'Floods' and 'Under the stairs' from *A Store of Candles*); and to the author ('Survivors', 'King William Park' and 'Incurables').

For poems by Tom Paulin: to Faber and Faber Ltd ('A September rising', 'In Antrim', 'Young funerals' and 'Bradley the last idealist' from *A State of Justice;* 'Still century', 'Anastasia McLaughlin', 'The garden of self-delight' and 'Where Art is a midwife' from *The Strange Museum*).

For poems by William Peskett: to Martin Secker and Warburg Ltd ('The nightowl', 'The question of time', 'Moths' and 'The inheritors' from *The Nightowl's Dissection*; 'From Belfast to Suffolk' and 'Cri de coeur' from *Survivors*); and to the author ('At Pamukkale').

For poems by Richard Ryan: to The Dolmen Press Ltd ('Famine village', 'Knockmany' and 'Father of Famine' from *Ledges*; 'Winter in Minneapolis' and 'From My Lai the thunder went west' from *Ravenswood*); and to the author ('God the Father').

For poems by Gerard Smyth: to New Writers' Press ('Forbidden knowledge' and 'The spirit of man' from *World Without End*); and to Raven Arts Press ('Builders' and 'Oracles' from *Loss and Gain*).

For poems by Matthew Sweeney: to Raven Arts Press ('Astronomy', 'Armada', 'The television creature speaks' and 'Funny face' from *A Dream of Maps*); and to the author ('The window').

For Poems by Patrick Williams: to Sidgwick and Jackson Ltd (*Trails*).

169

Some of the poems have appeared only in the following magazines and newspapers, to the editors of which acknowledgement is made: *Aquarius, The Honest Ulsterman,* 'New Irish Writing' (*The Irish Press*) and 'Writing in the West' (*The Connacht Tribune*).

I would also like to thank the Library staff of University College Galway and Kenny's Bookshop, Galway, for their help in the preparation of this book.

INDEX

173

Poets from the North of Ireland

George Buchanan   Louis MacNeice
Ciarán Carson   Derek Mahon
Gerald Dawe   Tom Matthews
Seamus Deane   John Montague
Padraic Fiacc   Paul Muldoon
Michael Foley   Frank Ormsby
Seamus Heaney   Tom Paulin
John Hewitt   William Peskett
Michael Longley   W.R. Rodgers
Roy McFadden   James Simmons

'*full of exquisite verbal pleasures*'   **Birmingham Post**

'*a rich and representative collection*'   **School Librarian**

'*It is a duty of the poet to defend private values in a time of public clamour, and one of the unexpected strengths of this anthology is its selection of love poems.*'   **TLS**

'*The richness which has resulted from the merging of two traditions is amply demonstrated in this splendid anthology*'   **Sunday Independent**

'*a large number of very good poems*'   **New Statesman**

ISBN 0 85640 201 X hb £6.50
ISBN 0 85640 135 8 pb £3.95